At Issue

Senior Citizens and Driving

Other Books in the At Issue Series:

Are Adoption Policies Fair?

Do Veterans Receive Adequate Health Care?

Foreign Oil Dependence

Guns and Crime

Has No Child Left Behind Been Good for Education?

How Does Advertising Impact Teen Behavior?

How Should the U.S. Proceed in Iraq?

National Security

Reality TV

Should Cameras Be Allowed in Courtrooms?

Should Drilling Be Permitted in the Arctic National
Wildlife Refuge?

Should Governments Negotiate with Terrorists?

Should Juveniles Be Tried as Adults?

Should the Legal Drinking Age Be Lowered?

Should Music Lyrics Be Censored for Violence
and Exploitation?

Should Parents Be Allowed to Choose the Gender
of Their Children?

Should Social Networking Web Sites Be Banned?

Teen Driving

At Issue

Senior Citizens and Driving

Tamara Thompson, Book Editor

GREENHAVEN PRESS
A part of Gale, Cengage Learning

 GALE
CENGAGE Learning

Detroit • New York • San Francisco • New Haven, Conn • Waterville, Maine • London

Christine Nasso, *Publisher*
Elizabeth Des Chenes, *Managing Editor*

© 2008 Greenhaven Press, a part of Gale, Cengage Learning.

Gale and Greenhaven Press are registered trademarks used herein under license.

For more information, contact:
Greenhaven Press
27500 Drake Rd.
Farmington Hills, MI 48331-3535
Or you can visit our Internet site at gale.cengage.com

For product information and technology assistance, contact us at

Gale Customer Support, 1-800-877-4253
For permission to use material from this text or product, submit all requests online at www.cengage.com/permissions

Further permissions questions can be emailed to permissionrequest@cengage.com

Articles in Greenhaven Press anthologies are often edited for length to meet page requirements. In addition, original titles of these works are changed to clearly present the main thesis and to explicitly indicate the author's opinion. Every effort is made to ensure that Greenhaven Press accurately reflects the original intent of the authors. Every effort has been made to trace the owners of copyrighted material.

Cover photograph reproduced by permission of Images.com/Corbis.

LIBRARY OF CONGRESS CATALOGING-IN-PUBLICATION DATA

Senior citizens and driving / Tamara Thompson, book editor.
    p. cm. -- (At issue)
Includes bibliographical references and index.
ISBN-13: 978-0-7377-4054-7 (hardcover)
ISBN-13: 978-0-7377-4055-4 (pbk.)
1. Older automobile drivers--United States. 2. Older people--United States
--Social conditions--21st century. 3. Older people--Transportation--United
States. 4. Traffic safety--United States. I. Thompson, Tamara.
HE5620.A24S46 2008
363.12'50846--dc22
                                                                2007050860

Printed in the United States of America
1 2 3 4 5 6 7 12 11 10 09 08

Contents

Introduction   7

1. Senior Drivers Are a Growing Public Danger   11
   Robert Davis and Anthony DeBarros

2. Seniors Are Safe Drivers   20
   *David S. Loughran, Seth A. Seabury and
   Laura Zakaras*

3. Society Must Balance Safety Concerns   29
   with the Needs of Senior Drivers
   Dr. Byron Thames

4. The Nation's Roads Increase Driving Dangers   35
   for Seniors
   Hal Karp

5. Seniors Who Stop Driving Decline   42
   Faster Than Those Who Still Drive
   SeniorJournal.com

6. More Seniors than Younger Drivers Die   46
   in Auto Accidents
   SeniorJournal.com

7. Seniors Who Cannot Drive Grapple   50
   with Isolation
   Gordon Dickson

8. Senior Drivers Should Be Screened   54
   More Thoroughly Than Others
   Katherine Siggerud

9. Taking Keys Away from Senior Drivers   60
   Is a Challenge for Families
   Janice Gallagher

10. The National Agenda Should Include   65
    Senior Driving Issues
    Ezra Ochshorn

11. Better Transit Programs Would Help   69
    Seniors Give Up Driving
    Helen Kerschner and Joan Harris

Organizations to Contact   83
Bibliography   90
Index   95

Introduction

When an eighty-six-year-old man hit the gas instead of the brake and plowed his Buick into a crowded farmer's market in Santa Monica, California, in 2003, he not only killed ten people and injured seventy, he also sparked a national debate about the safety of senior citizens behind the wheel. The elderly are the fastest growing age group in the country, and normal age-related declines in vision, cognitive ability, range of motion, attention span, coordination, and reaction time can all affect driving ability, as can health conditions and medication.

According to the U.S. Census Bureau, over the next three decades the number of Americans age sixty-five and older will double to nearly 70 million—more than twice the population of Canada. The force behind such explosive growth is the aging baby boom generation, the 76 million people born between 1946 and 1964. The boomers are the nation's largest demographic group, and the first members of this massive cohort have already entered their fifties; the last will turn fifty-five in 2019. By 2030, roughly 20 percent of the population will be over sixty-five, compared to less than 13 percent currently. The number of older drivers is expected to increase proportionally, right along with them.

Today, one in seven licensed drivers is sixty-five or older, but within twenty years that ratio will be almost one in four, according to the National Older Driver Research and Training Center. Additionally, the American Medical Association estimates that as the population ages, drivers over sixty-five will eventually be responsible for 25 percent of all auto fatalities. In 2005, just 11 percent of fatal crashes involved drivers that old. Senior advocates say that although these statistics are true, they greatly overstate the danger that older drivers pose because seniors are much more likely to be injured or die when they are in an accident than younger people are. Not only are vehicle accidents the leading cause of injury-related deaths among sixty-five- to seventy-four-year-olds and the second leading cause (after falls) among seventy-five- to eighty-four-year-olds, older drivers have a higher fatality rate per mile driven than any age group except drivers under twenty-five. What that means is that the danger senior drivers pose is mainly to themselves.

Nevertheless, high-profile cases—such as the Santa Monica incident and a bizarre 2005 case in which a ninety-three-year-old Florida man hit a pedestrian and continued driving with the man's body embedded in the car's windshield—have spurred a nationwide push for stricter licensing and testing procedures for senior drivers. The controversial point of whether age alone is an acceptable reason to test a driver more thoroughly is being argued in legislatures across the country as states weigh various options for addressing the issue.

While some studies suggest that having drivers renew their license in person is the only way to effectively identify those whose physical or mental ability has declined, most states do not require regular in-person renewals. Only two states—Illinois and New Hampshire—require behind the wheel tests for senior drivers (seventy-five and over), and no state has an age limit for driving. Critics argue that mandatory, age-based testing of older drivers has not been proven useful or cost-effective for identifying those who shouldn't be driving. They believe the idea is based on age discrimination, and they maintain that any license review should be triggered by concerns about an individual's health or driving behavior, not their age.

Many senior advocacy groups, such as the American Association of Retired Persons (AARP), strongly oppose efforts to impose stricter testing and licensing procedures for older drivers. They argue that better education, rather than legislation, is the key to preventing or minimizing many of the problems older drivers encounter. AARP offers a popular eight-hour Driver Safety Program to help drivers fifty and older sharpen their skills and learn about the effects of aging on driving. More than seven hundred thousand senior drivers complete the program annually. The organization's Web site, aarp.org, also offers advice for seniors and their families on how to stay safe on the road.

According to a 2002 study published in the *American Journal of Public Health,* most older drivers decide to stop driving on their own as their skills decline. More than six hundred thousand drivers seventy and over give up driving each year. But getting the next generation of seniors to voluntarily hang up the car keys may not be quite as easy. Baby boomers have particularly deep ties to America's car culture. They have lived primarily in suburban areas and depended on automobiles as the primary source of transportation throughout their lives. "This is a huge number of people, and they are people who were all born and raised with cars in their families," says Eero Laanso, human-factors engineer for Ford Motor Company. "They've led active lifestyles involving cars. And just because they reach a certain place in their lives, they're not going to say, 'I'm too old to drive now.'"

The primary reason that people do not want to stop driving even when they know they should is the fear of becoming socially isolated or dependent on others. Recent research shows that doing so may also have very real health consequences. A 2006 study by researchers at Johns Hopkins University found that seniors who continue driving are less likely to enter nursing homes or assisted living facilities than those who give up their car keys. The study found that nondrivers had four times the risk of entering long-term care than drivers did. The study's authors say they hope their findings will encourage communities to provide alternative transportation for seniors who cannot drive.

Indeed, the continued mobility of older adults is a growing focus for cities nationwide. City planners are paying increasing attention to the walkability and accessibility of their cities, and transportation planners are coming to understand that public transportation programs must be accessible and attractive to seniors, not just to able-bodied younger adults. A wide array of experimental transportation programs—from volunteer taxis, to ride-share programs, to senior vans—are being tried out in cities across the country.

Attention is also turning toward the nation's transportation infrastructure as a place to address the problem. Badly designed intersections, hard-to-read road signs, faded pavement markings, obstructed views and insufficient lighting all create road hazards that are particularly hard for senior drivers to overcome. Studies suggest that simple actions such as increasing the size of traffic signals, changing street signs to a more readable typeface, protecting cars making left turns in intersections, and improving lighting and road markings would all help reduce the problems seniors experience behind the wheel. The auto industry has a role to play as well. Automakers are making vehicles safer for seniors by improving crash safety, creating collision avoidance systems, paying attention to window views and seat height, and equipping cars with larger mirrors.

As the baby boom generation ages over the next three decades, the country will face major challenges as it responds to the changing needs of this uniquely large and mobile group. The authors in *At Issue: Senior Citizens and Driving* represent a wide range of viewpoints in the debates concerning the growing population of older drivers and how to balance their ongoing transportation needs with the need for public safety.

1

Senior Drivers Are a Growing Public Danger

Robert Davis and Anthony DeBarros

Robert Davis and Anthony DeBarros are staff writers for USA Today, *a daily newspaper with a national circulation.*

Dallas—As the baby boom generation ages, people over sixty-five will make up a larger part of the population. Consequently, there will be an increasing number of older drivers on the roads. Studies show that while older people are generally safe drivers, they are far more likely than a younger person to be injured or die when they get in an accident. Many seniors limit their driving as their skills decline and they eventually stop driving on their own. However, many others fiercely cling to the independence that driving represents and they continue driving longer than they safely should. Licensing requirements for seniors vary widely by state, and no one can predict which senior drivers will actually present a risk. As the public increasingly views senior drivers as a danger, the debate about how much states should do to screen them grows.

As his 90-year-old neighbor struggled last May [2006] to set out on a morning drive to the store, David Prager began to worry.

Elizabeth Grimes, a widow who had lived on Meaders Lane for 50 years, had backed out of her driveway, across her lawn and off the curb. Her 1994 Mercury Grand Marquis then hit the curb across the street, Prager recalls, before Grimes mistook the gas pedal for the brake and "took off with a jack-rabbit start."

INTERACTIVE: How aging affects the ability to drive.

RESTRICTIONS: A state-by-state look at the laws.

WARNING SIGNS: When is it time to put brakes on the elderly?

Six blocks away, Grimes drove through a red light. The car slammed into Katie Bolka, a 17-year-old high school junior who was driving to school to take an algebra test. Five days later, Bolka died.

The crash was emblematic of what health and safety analysts say is likely to be an increasing problem as the elderly population booms: aging drivers, clinging to the independence that cars give them but losing their ability to operate the vehicles, causing more accidents.

Fatality rates for drivers begin to climb after age 65, according to a recent study by Carnegie Mellon University in Pittsburgh and the AAA [American Automobile Association] Foundation for Traffic Safety, based on data from 1999–2004. From ages 75 to 84, the rate of about three deaths per 100 million miles driven is equal to the death rate of teenage drivers. For drivers 85 and older, the fatality rate skyrockets to nearly four times higher than that for teens.

Most state driver's license laws require basic eye exams but typically cannot detect a driver's diminished physical capacity and cognitive awareness. No state has an age limit on drivers.

The numbers are particularly daunting at a time when the U.S. Census Bureau projects there will be 9.6 million people 85 and older by 2030, up 73% from today. Road safety analysts predict that by 2030, when all baby boomers are at least

65, they will be responsible for 25% of all fatal crashes. In 2005, 11% of fatal crashes involved drivers that old.

Debates over how to prepare for a boom in elderly drivers are resonating in statehouses across the nation—including Texas, where Bolka's death has inspired the Legislature to pass a measure that could lead to more frequent vision tests and behind-the-wheel exams for drivers 79 and older.

The only measure scientifically proven to lower the rate of fatal crashes involving elderly drivers is forcing the seniors to appear at motor vehicle departments in person to renew their licenses, says the Insurance Institute for Highway Safety (IIHS), citing a 1995 study in the *Journal of the American Medical Association*.

But most states do not require older drivers to renew licenses in person, and only two—Illinois and New Hampshire—require them to pass road tests, which can be crucial in identifying drivers whose physical ability or mental awareness has diminished.

States have tried a range of approaches, but for the most part they have struggled to establish precise standards for determining when seniors should be kept off the road while being fair to older drivers who remain capable.

State laws are inconsistent on the issue, according to the IIHS, which researches factors that cause crashes. Most state driver's license laws require basic eye exams but typically cannot detect a driver's diminished physical capacity and cognitive awareness. No state has an age limit on drivers.

"It's a huge problem, and we really don't have any solutions to it yet," says Barbara Harsha, executive director of the Governors Highway Safety Association. "We need to keep moving on it and try to find solutions as quickly as possible."

Safety and health specialists are especially concerned about drivers 85 and older, who, federal crash statistics show, are involved in three fatal accidents a day.

"You always hear about teenage (driver) risks being so incredibly high, but to me the amazing thing is there are two clusters you really have to focus on": teens and elderly drivers, says Paul Fischbeck of the Center for the Study and Improvement of Regulation at Carnegie Mellon.

Normal aging causes medical problems that affect driving. Reflexes, flexibility, visual acuity, memory and the ability to focus all decline with age. Medicines that treat various ailments also make it more difficult to focus and make snap decisions.

Elderly drivers are less likely than other drivers to be in crashes involving high speeds or alcohol, but they are more likely to crash at intersections where they miss a stop sign or turn left in front of oncoming traffic.

"Where single-vehicle rollovers can be described as a young person's crash, side impact appears to be an old person's crash," National Highway Traffic Safety Administration researchers Rory Austin and Barbara Faigin wrote in a 2003 study of crash occupants published in the *Journal of Safety Research*.

Crashes Shine a Spotlight

Even so, a series of incidents involving elderly drivers in the past few years has fueled the debate over how to deal with the risks they can pose.Among them:

George Russell Weller, then 86, killed 10 people and injured more than 70 when he drove his Buick Le Sabre into a crowded farmers market in Santa Monica, Calif., on July 16, 2003.

His attorneys explained that Weller had confused his car's accelerator for the brake. He was convicted of vehicular manslaughter with gross negligence.

A judge ruled that Weller was too ill to be imprisoned and sentenced him to probation and $101,700 in penalties. The case fueled a nationwide debate over how elderly drivers should be screened.

Brian Fay, 19, was making change for a customer at a Sears store in Orlando on Oct. 9 [2006] when he heard what he thought was a bomb. Fay looked toward the store entrance and saw a pane of glass shatter and fall to the floor. Then he "looked down and saw (a) car barreling" toward him.

Elizabeth Jane Baldick, 84, drove her car into the cash register counter Fay was using, knocking him over. Bleeding, he rushed to check on Baldick, whose car had come to rest against a concrete pillar. Her foot was still pressed firmly against the accelerator, the tires screeching against the tiles on the floor.

Florida revoked Baldick's driving privileges in December [2006], citing medical reasons, says Kim Miller of the Florida Highway Patrol.

Most elderly drivers decide to stop driving themselves. More than 600,000 drivers age 70 and older decide to give up driving each year.

The Grimes accident in Dallas is typical of many crashes involving elderly drivers, health and safety specialists say: It involved someone who was reluctant to give up her car keys, and who drove mostly on familiar roads near her home.

Elinor Ginzler, AARP's director of livable communities, says the elderly can "suffer because they are stuck at home" after giving up their keys. So they drive for as long as they can by going only where they must as their skills diminish.

"Many elderly drivers do what we call 'self-regulate,'" says Ginzler, whose association for seniors encourages its members to assess when they should give up driving. "They only drive to the places that they know, on familiar roads, at certain times of the day."

As long as a driver can navigate such trips safely, "those are very, very good decisions to be making," she says. "Making a decision (not to) drive at night anymore is terrific. It means you recognize this isn't safe anymore."

AARP offers a Driver Safety Program at sites around the country and online.

The program is an eight-hour class for drivers 50 and older that deals with the effects of aging on driving. The organization's website, aarp.org, also offers advice for seniors and their adult children on how to stay safe.

Most elderly drivers decide to stop driving themselves. More than 600,000 drivers age 70 and older decide to give up driving each year, according to a 2002 study published in the *American Journal of Public Health*.

That's partly why insurance rates usually are only slightly higher for drivers 75 or older—and far lower than such rates for teenage drivers. Insurance analysts say the car insurance industry does not see a big liability threat from the rising number of elderly drivers because such drivers hurt themselves more than others and tend to stop driving on their own.

"When they realize they are driving in dangerous conditions they generally stop doing it," says Carolyn Gorman, vice president of the Insurance Information Institute, based in New York City.

"The industry views them as pretty much a self-policing group. Many elderly drivers do not drive at night. Many will make three right-hand turns instead of one left-hand turn."

Grimes, who died Jan. 15 [2001] from what Dallas County medical examiner Richard Baer says were complications from a stroke and old age, had cooked her own meals, cleaned her house and mowed her lawn—which she called her therapy.

Through their attorney, her family members declined to discuss her driving. But Grimes said after the crash that she frequently had made short trips around her neighborhood.

"I'm not going at any high rate of speed because I'm here, there and yonder along the way," she said about three months after the crash in a videotaped deposition for a lawsuit filed by Bolka's family. "This is my area."

Grimes' family members say they suspect she had a mild stroke the night before the crash that fatally injured Bolka, and the stroke caused a sudden decline in Grimes' ability to drive safely.

The lawsuit filed by the Bolkas was settled on Sept. 14 [2006] for an undisclosed amount.

Harsha says no state has a good "early warning system" when it comes to identifying elderly drivers in declining health.

The burden rests on spouses, family members, doctors and police to request that a license be revoked. Appealing for a state to revoke someone's driver's license on medical grounds is a cumbersome process, and such requests are rare.

What States Are Doing

Twenty-three states require licensed drivers of a certain age to appear periodically at a department of motor vehicles office to renew their license. In 16 states, older drivers must prove that they can see well enough to drive. Some states have tried other ways to identify drivers who, because of age-related health problems, put themselves or others at risk.

But the IIHS says such efforts have failed to accurately predict the risk an elderly driver may pose.

Without precise measures, analysts estimate that 500 good drivers would have to be taken off the road to prevent a single crash. Among states' efforts to restrict elderly drivers:

- California tested a three-tiered pilot plan for assessing drivers of all ages that included a driving knowledge test, cognitive screening and vision tests. People who failed the first tiers had to pass a road test. The 2003 study of 152 drivers did not predict who would go on to have a crash.

- Maryland conducted a study that found drivers who performed poorly on certain cognitive tests—such as following basic commands and repeating simple movements—were about 25% more likely than others to go on to cause a crash. Results of the study of 1,910 drivers ages 55 to 96 were published in January 2006 in the *Journal of the American Geriatrics Society.*

- Maryland now uses such screening on a regular basis with drivers whose actions raise concerns about their cognitive abilities.

- Florida's requirement that drivers 80 and older pass a vision test resulted in the loss of a license for about 7% of elderly drivers seeking renewal, according to a study by the IIHS.

But nearly 20% of those 80 and older who needed to renew their license told researchers they decided to give up driving because they did not think they could pass the vision test.

"We don't know for sure if any of these (efforts) will prevent fatal crashes," says Russ Rader of the IIHS.

"But having drivers go in person for renewal allows the examiner to see the person and spot impairments. That can be effective."

'I Did It. I'm Terribly Sorry'

David Prager, Grimes' former neighbor in Dallas, says there was little he could do to keep her off the road. "There was no way Mrs. Grimes was going to stop driving," Prager says.

Grimes said in her deposition—taken in the nursing home where she went after suffering two broken ankles in the accident that killed Bolka—that she "never had a reason until now" to discuss giving up her car.

Just before the fatal crash, Grimes' car had suffered front-end damage after an accident in a parking lot at the same intersection where Grimes struck Bolka.

"I had it repaired," she said in her deposition. "Everything was happy."

Bolka's family members say they pushed the Texas Legislature to pass the bill toughening the state's laws on bad elderly drivers because they believe states should be more aggressive in keeping such drivers off the road.

Right now, "the first level of defense is the driver," says Rick Bolka, Katie's father. "The second level of defense is the (driver's) family. The third level of defense is the (driver's) physician. We would like to see the state become the first level of defense. The government has a responsibility to protect its citizens."

Texas Sen. John Corona, R-Dallas, the Bolkas' state senator, said during a recent hearing that his mother "is blind, and they just renewed her license by mail."

The bill, which is scheduled to be signed soon by Texas Gov. Rick Perry, would require drivers 79 and older to appear in person for renewals and subject them to mandatory vision tests and behind-the-wheel exams if officials have any question about their driving ability. Drivers 85 and older would be required to renew every two years.

During his deposition of Grimes, the Bolka family's attorney, Peter Malouf, asked Grimes whether she understood that she had crashed into a young girl's car and killed her.

"I'm aware of that very sad story, yes," Grimes said. "Sure I did it. I'm terribly sorry. But I did it."

Malouf asked whether there was anything she would like to say to the family.

"What is there to say to people who have been hurt?" Grimes said. "That's best left alone, I think."

2

Seniors Are Safe Drivers

David S. Loughran, Seth A. Seabury, and Laura Zakaras

David Loughran is a professor of economics at the University of Maryland. Seth Seabury is a professor of law and economics at Columbia University. Laura Zakaras is a professor of policy analysis at the University of Washington.

This research study shows that—contrary to popular belief—older drivers pose only a slightly higher risk than adult drivers, and are not nearly as dangerous as teens behind the wheel. Because the worst senior drivers encounter pressure from family and others to quit driving, many curtail their driving or cease entirely. Such self-regulation means that only the healthiest and safest older drivers remain on the road. Because of this factor, the oldest driver of the four groups studied (those over seventy) were actually the safest drivers of all, causing only half the accidents of the fifty-five and older group. The researchers also found that the main risk older drivers pose is to themselves. Senior drivers are 573 times more likely to die when they are in a crash than a younger adult is.

Policymakers, insurers, and the public have long been concerned about the effects of aging on the ability to operate a motor vehicle safely. Under the assumption that older drivers are more dangerous than are younger drivers, many states impose stricter licensing requirements on older drivers. As the proportion of licensed drivers 65 and older continues to in-

David S. Loughran, Seth A. Seabury, and Laura Zakaras, *Regulating Older Drivers: Are New Policies Needed?* Santa Monica, CA: RAND Corporation, 2007. © Copyright 2007 RAND Corporation. All rights reserved. Republished with permission of the RAND Corporation, conveyed through Copyright Clearance Center, Inc.

crease, states may impose additional licensing requirements on older drivers in an attempt to lessen the threat that older drivers pose to traffic safety.

This . . . viewpoint presents new evidence on the threat that older drivers pose to traffic safety and discusses what this new evidence implies for public policy. . . .

In July 2003, an 86-year-old man drove his 1982 Buick into a crowd of pedestrians shopping at an open-air farmers' market in Santa Monica, California, killing 10 and injuring more than 50. In October 2005, a 93-year-old man struck a pedestrian in St. Petersburg, Florida, and did not notice the corpse hanging out his windshield until a tollbooth operator stopped him. Shocking incidents such as these have reinvigorated a long-simmering debate over the riskiness of older drivers and led to calls for stricter state licensing policies for these drivers. The issue is particularly important in light of demographic projections: By 2025, drivers 65 and older will represent 25 percent of the driving population, compared to 15 percent in 2001.

Although it has been scientifically established that physical and cognitive degeneration at older ages compromises driving ability, it is not clear just how much riskier older drivers are than other drivers. Most published research shows that accidents per mile driven increase when drivers are in their fifties and, by the time they reach their eighties, accidents per mile driven are almost as high as they are for the youngest drivers. As we describe later, however, this measure of risk can be misleading. . . .

Physical Changes Come with Aging

Medical research has demonstrated that, as people age, their driving ability becomes impaired. The most common problem is declining eyesight: Glaucoma, macular degeneration, and cataracts—all of which become more common with age— reduce night and peripheral vision and vision acuity and cause individuals to become more sensitive to glare. Impaired vision is strongly associated with a greater likelihood of causing an accident among older drivers. Normal changes in brain functioning slow reflex reactions and reduce the ability to take in information from disparate sources simultaneously. Severe changes in brain functioning, such as depression and dementia, as well as the medications used to treat those illnesses, may seriously hamper an older person's ability to drive. Other common afflictions of older people—heart disease, arthritis, and insomnia, for example—can also reduce driving skills.

There is also evidence, however, that older individuals compensate for their impairment by changing their driving behavior. Many older drivers drive less frequently, and, when they do drive, they tend to avoid high-speed zones and driving at night. Eventually, most older individuals decide to stop driving altogether, either because they recognize that they are likelier to cause an accident or because a family member or doctor urges them to stop driving. To identify the appropriate policy response to older drivers, such self-regulation must be taken into account.

Because older drivers pose such a large risk to themselves, the riskiest older drivers choose to curtail their driving the most, leaving safer older drivers on the road.

Many states have already responded to the perceived risk posed by older drivers by creating stiffer licensing requirements as drivers age. Some states require older drivers to renew their licenses in person and with greater frequency than younger drivers and to pass vision tests at renewal. Fewer states require older drivers to pass written tests and require older drivers to take road tests. Should more DMVs [Departments of Motor Vehicles] adopt road tests for older individuals or, as AARP [American Association of Retired Persons] recommends, generally devote more resources to screening older drivers for competency and provide remedial training and education to those who need it.

Study Purpose and Approach

To inform the policy debate surrounding older drivers, our study sought to answer four related questions:

- How much likelier are older drivers than other drivers to cause a crash?

- How much less do older drivers drive than other drivers do?

- How much more vulnerable are they than other drivers to being injured or killed in accidents?

- To what extent do older drivers take steps on their own to mitigate the risks of driving? . . .

There are relatively few older drivers who need to be legally prohibited from driving, so these drivers pose a relatively small risk to traffic safety overall.

For our purposes, we examined two-car crashes between pairs of drivers from three age groups: younger drivers (15 to 24 years old), adult drivers (25 to 64 years old), and older drivers (65 and older). Knowing the age group of the driver of each car in two-car fatal crashes (e.g., two older drivers, two adult drivers, one adult driver and one older driver), we could estimate the relative riskiness of older drivers, the relative amount they drive (to which we refer as their *relative exposure*), and their relative likelihood of being killed in a car accident (to which we refer as their *relative fragility*). . . .

What the Research Found

We found that drivers 65 and older are slightly likelier (specifically, 16 percent likelier) than adult drivers to cause an accident. Young drivers, on the other hand, are 188 percent likelier than adult drivers to cause an accident. We also found that older drivers and their passengers are nearly seven times likelier than adult drivers and their passengers to be killed in an accident. This could help explain why, despite medical evidence that suggests that driving ability should decline with age, the older individuals who do drive are not much more dangerous than middle-aged drivers. Because older drivers pose such a large risk to themselves, the riskiest older drivers choose to curtail their driving the most, leaving safer older drivers on the road.

Coverage of the older-driver issue in the popular press has largely focused on the very oldest drivers (e.g., 75 and older). While we find that drivers 70 and older are no riskier than drivers 65 and older, we are unable to examine with our methods the riskiness of the very oldest drivers. We note, however, that, while riskiness may increase at such advanced ages, there are very few of these drivers on the road, so their overall contribution to accident rates is likely to be small.

Altogether, these findings suggest that state DMVs should carefully weigh the costs and benefits of imposing stricter licensing requirements on older drivers. On the one hand, requiring older drivers to take road tests, for example, would certainly identify some older drivers whose driving abilities have deteriorated unacceptably. But our results suggest that there are relatively few older drivers who need to be legally prohibited from driving, so these drivers pose a relatively small risk to traffic safety overall. And the costs of requiring all older drivers to take such a test are not insignificant, either in terms of staffing resources or in terms of the stigma that older drivers might experience as a result of being singled out solely on the basis of age.

Nonetheless, automobile travel is clearly dangerous for older drivers and passengers because they are more susceptible to injury. Policies that promote safer automobile design, offer alternatives to automobile travel, and reduce the riskiness of younger drivers (who are far likelier to cause an accident both because they are riskier and because they drive more) could help stem the rise in injuries and fatalities that is likely to occur with an aging population. . . .

The objective of stricter licensing requirements and other policies targeting older drivers is to make the roads safer for all. But, to debate whether such policies are needed, we need to answer the following questions: How much likelier are older drivers than other drivers to cause a crash? How much less do older drivers drive than other drivers do? How much more vulnerable are they than other drivers to being injured or killed in accidents? To what extent do older drivers take steps on their own to mitigate the risks of driving?

The Relative Riskiness and Exposure of Older Drivers

Our most important finding is that older drivers are not that much riskier than adult drivers and far less risky than young adult drivers. Older drivers are 16 percent likelier to cause a crash than adult drivers are. While that difference is significant, it is perhaps far smaller than the conventional wisdom, fueled by anecdote, would imply that it would be. And it is nowhere near the risk that younger drivers pose to the public. . . . The youngest drivers are 188 percent likelier than adult drivers to cause a crash.

Older drivers are 573 percent likelier to be killed in a crash than adult drivers are.

We also find that older drivers drive far less than adult drivers do. . . . On average, older drivers drive 38 percent fewer miles than do adult drivers. Younger drivers, on the other hand, drive about 54 percent more miles than adult drivers do.

Together, these findings suggest that younger drivers pose a much greater risk to traffic safety than do older drivers, both because they are likelier to cause a crash and because they drive many more miles. By our estimates, older drivers, who represent 15 percent of all licensed drivers, cause 7 percent of all two-car accidents (both fatal and nonfatal). Younger drivers, on the other hand, who represent 13 percent of all licensed drivers, cause 43 percent of all two-car accidents.

The Relative Fragility of Older Drivers

If older drivers are only slightly likelier to cause an accident than are adult drivers, then why do they appear to be at such a high risk of being in a fatal accident? The answer to this question can be found by examining the difference in the probability that older drivers will be killed in a crash. . . . Older drivers are 573 percent likelier to be killed in a crash than adult drivers are, while younger drivers are 44 percent likelier to be killed than adult drivers are. We suspect, but cannot verify, that older drivers are also much likelier to sustain a nonfatal injury when involved in an accident.

Older drivers pose only a slightly increased risk to other drivers. The main danger they pose on the road is not to others but to themselves.

The Self-Regulation of Older Drivers

Our findings on the relative riskiness of older drivers are somewhat counterintuitive. Why, one might ask, do older drivers not appear riskier, given medical evidence that establishes that their driving skill declines with age? We propose that the answer is that older drivers change their driving habits to compensate for their diminished competence behind the wheel. Our analysis suggests that this self-regulation takes several forms.

First, many drivers simply cease driving at older ages because they pose an elevated risk to others and to themselves. The most dangerous drivers face pressure to stop driving from a number of sources, including state regulations, family members, and their own survival instinct or self-interest. If older drivers are responsive to this pressure, then we might expect those at the greatest risk of causing an accident to remove themselves from the pool of drivers, leaving behind older drivers who drive comparatively well. Since our analysis is based on data about older drivers who continue to drive, our results will reflect this self-regulation.

Additional findings support this conjecture. . . . Our results change as we vary the group of drivers we define as *older* from 55 and older to 70 and older. As the group ages, the risk of being killed in a crash increases significantly, but the risk of causing a crash declines. In fact, the very oldest drivers are the *least* likely of all the four groups of older drivers to cause a crash—and half as likely as the group 55 and older. This result also defies conventional wisdom, which holds that the older the driver, the greater the risk that driver poses to other drivers. But it is consistent with the idea that the population of drivers becomes more competent with age because the worst drivers stop driving. Only the healthiest and safest older drivers remain on the road at very old ages.

Second, our analysis offers evidence that older drivers avoid road conditions that put them at greater risk. For example, evidence suggests that, at advanced age, drivers find it more difficult to drive at rush hour and at night. If older drivers regulate their driving to promote safety, we would expect them to drive less during the peak daytime and nighttime hours. The results . . . confirm that assumption. Here, we plot changes in the exposure of older and younger drivers on the road at different times of day relative to their exposure at noon. We present the results as relative to noon to control for the fact that exposure is mechanically higher for younger drivers (because there are more of them), so it is easier to compare the two series this way. . . . Older drivers tend to stay off the road during peak traffic times and appear most prevalent during off-peak daytime hours, particularly between 10:00 a.m. and noon. By contrast, younger drivers show no particular pattern during the day but drive more frequently at night.

Risk Is Only Slight

In summary, we find that older drivers are only slightly likelier than other drivers to cause an accident but are considerably likelier to be killed in one. Younger drivers, on the other hand, are considerably likelier than other drivers to cause a crash, drive much more frequently than older drivers, and are less susceptible to fatal injuries than older drivers are. These findings do not mean that driving skills do not, in fact, deteriorate with age as a result of worsening mental and physical impairments. Instead, our evidence suggests that older drivers adjust their behavior in light of these worsening impairments. Many older drivers cease to drive altogether; many others reduce the miles they drive and avoid the most dangerous driving conditions. Because they are aware of their own limitations and adjust their driving patterns in response, older drivers pose only a slightly increased risk to other drivers. The main danger they pose on the road is not to others but to themselves.

3

Society Must Balance Safety Concerns with the Needs of Senior Drivers

Dr. Byron Thames

Dr. Byron Thames is on the board of directors of the AARP, the American Association of Retired Persons, a nationwide senior advocacy group with more than 35 million members age fifty and older.

Society should be concerned not only about seniors who drive, but also about those who have stopped driving. When seniors stop driving, they face many hardships. They may become isolated because they are cut off from social activity. Their health may decline because they cannot get to doctor's appointments or the pharmacy. They may be afraid to alienate family and friends by asking for rides. They may become sad and depressed and their quality of life may suffer. Transportation policy should shift away from automobiles and toward public transportation to support the needs of this growing segment of the population.

Nationally, we're just a few years away from a dramatic demographic shift. The baby boom generation is getting older. The latest predictions say that by the year 2030, one in five Americans will be 65 or older. And at least three-fourths of all members of that group will be licensed drivers.

As bad as traffic is today, it isn't likely to get any better as our population ages. Older people prefer using private ve-

Dr. Byron Thames, "Keeping Our Eyes on the Road: How an Aging Population Will Get from Here to There," Speech to The Florida Council on Aging Mobility Challenges Panel in Orlando, FL, www.aarp.org, August 24, 2005. Reproduced by permission.

hicles more than any other mode of transportation. They make nearly 90 percent of their trips in a private vehicle, either as a passenger or driver. And they do this even when public transit is affordable and available.

In Florida, the number of drivers over the age of 65 is expected to increase even faster than the age 65 plus population itself. Here in Orlando, with its constant influx of retirees, we can already see a sharp increase in older drivers on our roads. We're becoming more aware that these older drivers must deal with gradual changes in functioning, changes in their reflexes, their ability to make quick decisions, their vision at night. Changes that can have a definite impact on driving.

Seniors Are Typically Safe Drivers

Because of these changes, many older drivers begin to monitor themselves. Some stop driving at night. Others choose to use only familiar roads during off-peak hours. And, for the most part, older individuals are safe drivers. As a group, they have lower rates of crashes than younger drivers; they have the lowest percentage of crashes involving alcohol and the highest rate of seatbelt use of any age group.

But, even so, Florida, which leads the country in the number of older residents and older drivers, also leads the country in the number of fatal automobile accidents involving drivers over the age of 75.

Non-drivers over the age of 75 say they face severe restrictions on their daily activities.

This increased incidence of fatal crashes can be attributed mostly to increased fragility, which makes people 75 and older more likely to be killed or injured in a crash. But it can also be attributed, in part, to the driving environment—complicated intersections, hard to read signs, badly timed traffic lights.

Along with our causes for concern about the gradual changes in elderly drivers, we also need to pay attention to the gradual changes in those people over 65, 75, and 85 who have given up driving. Because driving cessation may result in losing community mobility.

What Happens When Seniors Stop Driving?

As a family doctor, I can tell you firsthand what happens when seniors lose their independence and are stranded without adequate transportation options. It's not just a matter of a little inconvenience. They become sedentary and isolated, and it sucks the life right out of them—literally and figuratively.

It cuts them off from family, social opportunities and civic activities. It makes it harder to go to the doctor or the pharmacy. It too often leads to depression, obesity, even alcoholism, and declining health in general.

I've seen it in my practice, but I'm sure many of you . . . also know a relative, friend or neighbor who's gone from vibrant and vigorous to sad and lethargic, simply because they have no easy way to get around.

The baby boomers are the most mobile generation in the history of civilization.

One of AARP's [American Association of Retired Persons] most recent studies found that non-drivers over the age of 75 say they face severe restrictions on their daily activities. In fact, they were six times as likely as drivers to miss doing something they would have liked to do because they did not have the transportation.

America's Car Culture

The mobility challenge will be that much greater when it comes to this current wave of aging Americans. Not just because of their large numbers and their long life expectancy . . . but because the baby boomers are the most mobile generation in the history of civilization.

They've lived their entire adult lives in a society where driving and living are practically one and the same. Think about it. If you're turning 60 this year, it means you grew up steeped in the car-crazed consumerism of postwar America. It means you were getting your license when the interstate highway system was being built. It means your attitudes and values were being shaped at just the moment that the car was becoming a powerful cultural icon denoting status and independence.

These folks are attached to their cars. They want to extend their driving lives as long as they possibly can. And we should do everything we can to help them.

AARP is one of several organizations that offer Driver Safety Programs. [About] 700,000 people a year complete the AARP course, where they learn to adjust their driving behavior to stay safe and confident as they experience the vision changes and slower reaction times that are a normal part of aging.

But for many elderly people—and it will probably happen to many more in the coming decades—there comes that day when they have to hand over the keys.

Then what?

As a society and as individual communities, we have to be ready.

Public Transportation Policy Must Change

But as a nation, we don't yet have a truly multimodal transportation vision. Other nations, like Sweden for example, begin their planning with the assumption that one form of transportation can't possibly serve the entire community.

But here in the U.S., 60 years of federal transportation policy has focused almost exclusively on the construction and maintenance of roads to accommodate the automobile. That mind-set has to change.

We need more pedestrian-safe communities. Remember sidewalks? Sometimes it seems like they've gone the way of the Studebaker [a popular midcentury American automobile]. So many neighborhoods are designed to make walking as unpleasant and dangerous as possible, especially if you're older and you don't move so quickly.

There can be no dignity or purpose without the ability to get from here to there.

We need aggressive investment in our mass transit systems. In a recent survey we conducted at AARP, 60 percent of seniors said that there was no public transportation within 10-minute walking distance of their homes. The suburbs and rural areas are badly underserved in this area. And even many urban public transportation systems are geared toward commuters, offering infrequent service during off-peak hours or to areas where there aren't many offices and workplaces. We need greater innovation—more feeder routes, more dial-a-ride options, and more hybrid services.

Solutions Will Take Funding and Effort

And by the way, public transportation shouldn't just be seen as a last resort when driving is no longer an option. It should be prevalent enough in our communities that people are accustomed to using it regularly throughout their lives.

We also need to do more to encourage specialized transportation operated by human service agencies and non-profits. That includes clearing barriers that keep these agencies from obtaining insurance to cover volunteer drivers.

It's going to take more public dollars. It's going to take grassroots activism from the citizens who live with the consequences of these decisions every day. And it's going to take an increased commitment from our policymakers.

At AARP, our vision is to help Americans 50 and over age with dignity and purpose. But there can be no dignity or purpose without the ability to get from here to there. Increasing the options for mobility and transportation is at the heart of AARP's 10-year social impact agenda. Meeting the needs of an aging population, keeping them safe as drivers and then mobile and independent when they stop driving—these are all part of our program.

The challenge is an awesome one, but we have no choice. We have to do it if we want to stay true to universal American values like freedom, dignity and choice.

4

The Nation's Roads Increase Driving Dangers for Seniors

Hal Karp

Hal Karp is a reporter for Reader's Digest, *a monthly general interest magazine.*

While aging does cause physical changes that affect driving ability, perhaps the biggest contributor to senior driving accidents is the nation's poor transportation infrastructure. Badly designed intersections, hard-to-read road signs, faded pavement markings, obstructed views, and insufficient lighting all create road hazards that are particularly difficult for senior drivers to overcome. Studies suggest that simple steps such as increasing the size of traffic signals, changing street signs to a more readable typeface, protecting cars making left turns in intersections, equipping cars with larger mirrors and improving lighting and road markings would help improve driving safety for seniors as well as the general public.

On a crisp fall morning in October [2002], Sandy Johnson, 46, and her mother buckled up and headed out to pick apples on a farm in Licking County, Ohio. The two were traveling east on Morse Road and approaching the intersection at Route 310 when Sandy noticed a red-flashing signal light and stop sign. The mother of two brought her car to a halt, and then pulled out. She didn't make it far.

A Chevrolet Blazer, heading down Route 310 at 55 m.p.h. [miles per hour], seemingly materialized from nowhere to crash broadside into Sandy's Mazda 626. Her skull was crushed, her spine was snapped and her lungs and heart were ripped open. Her 71-year-old mother, her neck broken, took her last breath.

Sandy and her husband, Dean, 57, had been preparing to celebrate their 23rd wedding anniversary. After a highway patrolman delivered the worst of all news, Dean says, "In an instant, the love of my life was ripped from my soul."

Because he knew Sandy was a safe driver, Johnson looked to the intersection for answers. He discovered nearly 70 crashes had occurred there from 1990 to 1999. In the past 13 years, the Ohio Department of Transportation (ODOT) had conducted six studies of the site, culminating with a 50-page report in August 2001, more than a year before Sandy and her mother were killed.

Officials concluded that the main problem was a corner house that cut the view to about one-quarter of what would be an adequate distance. Putting up a traffic signal would reduce collisions by an estimated 80 percent. But the crossroads didn't meet certain criteria, so the signal was ruled out.

"Crash rates for this group continue to climb because existing road hazards and aging don't mix well."

In April 2002, ODOT requested and received approval to purchase and raze the view-obstructing house. But at the time of Sandy's collision, the project remained unscheduled. ODOT says that due to the size of the state's highway network, it just can't fix everything at once.

Dean Johnson's crusade to make the intersection safe, however, spurred change. By mid-December [2002], a four-way stop was installed as an interim measure and a full traffic signal is planned.

Intersection accidents like Sandy's are all too common. According to the National Highway Traffic Safety Administration

(NHTSA), nearly half of all reported crashes in 2001 were related to intersections. That's 2.7 million collisions a year. Intersections are not the only hazard either.

Across America's 4 million miles of blacktop, every day a multitude of dangers awaits you and your vehicle: poorly designed and outdated roads, shoddily maintained thoroughfares, inadequate signs and lighting, and a lack of safe crosswalks for pedestrians. The simple truth is that you can buy the safest car available, drive carefully, and still be in danger because the road itself is working against you.

"We've done a great deal over the past couple of decades to improve driver and vehicle safety," says Diane Steed, former head of NHTSA and now executive director of the Roadway Safety Foundation (RSF). "But our roads are not safe enough, and it's time to bring this to the floor."

But fixing problems gets expensive quickly. And in times of tight budgets, states and localities are often left without enough to do the job.

Meanwhile, road use is soaring. In 2000, Americans traveled 2.7 trillion miles, up 20 percent since 1993. And experts are becoming concerned about who's behind the wheel. Bella Dinh-Zarr, national director of traffic safety policy for AAA [Automobile Associaton of America], points out that by 2020 there will be more than 40 million licensed drivers over the age of 65. "Crash rates for this group continue to climb because existing road hazards and aging don't mix well."

Dangerous Crossings

Reader's Digest wondered how often roadway designs and defects might contribute to serious accidents, so we analyzed NHTSA fatal crash data from 1998 to 2001, removing accidents linked to driver error or impairment. The result: 24,067 people were killed. One-third of them were at intersections, where confusing lanes, blind spots and inadequate signs can cause havoc.

"Left-turning vehicles are involved in the worst kinds of crashes and those most often associated with fatalities and serious injuries," says Richard Miller, manager of community safety services for AAA Michigan. Aging boomers face special problems in these maneuvers. Starting in their 60s, many people will lose some of their ability to judge the speed of oncoming cars. Complex judgments, like executing a quick left turn, can take these drivers 50 percent more time than they take a 20-year-old.

Starting in 1996, AAA Michigan began working with city officials in Detroit and Grand Rapids to reduce crashes at hazardous intersections. A big part of the program: the addition of left-hand turn lanes with their own signals. Says Miller, "Protecting a person making a left turn really drops the probability of a crash."

Other changes included increasing the size of traffic signals from 8- to 12-inch lenses, placing signals over each lane and adding all-red intervals. "When your light turns red, it's still red in all other directions for a second or two. It allows the intersection to clear," Miller explains.

Injuries at some crossings were slashed by as much as 71 percent. Overall, the intersections in Detroit experienced a 47 percent reduction. Results in Grand Rapids were comparable. Over 130 intersections in the two cities have been upgraded; by the end of next year [2004], all 300 known problematic intersections will have been enhanced.

Design or Default?

On Thanksgiving [2002], 17-year-old Chad Sutton and his best friend were cruising down FM 2869 in Wood County, Texas, when they struck a deer that had jumped onto the road. As Chad's 1998 Trans Am ricocheted to the right, he overcorrected, swerving to the left. The car collided with a guardrail shielding vehicles from a 40-foot drop. The safety device's sloped end acted as a ramp and launched the sports car. It flipped four times on its way to the bottom. Chad died from massive trauma; his friend suffered a head wound. Both were wearing seat belts.

At the scene it was clear the guardrail had contributed to the crash. Chad's mother, Risa Sutton, 47, learned that three decades earlier federal experts had determined that such guardrails were unacceptable because of accidents like her son's. In fact, in 1990, new installation of these guardrails was forbidden on high-speed, high-volume roads receiving federal aid.

But FM 2869 was not high-volume, and so when the guardrail near the Suttons' home was installed in June 1999, the old design was used. Three years later, the Texas Department of Transportation (TxDOT) moved forward with new standards for all state roads, regardless of speed or volume, but the decision came too late for Chad Sutton.

"It takes time and money to change gears," explains Ken Bohuslav, the director of TxDOT's design division. Existing guardrails are not replaced unless other work is being done at the site.

At nighttime, signs and pavement markings increase in importance.

"Roads need to be forgiving, not punishing," says RSF's Steed. "They need to allow you to compensate and recover from mistakes. Too many roads fail on this measure." Other unforgiving hazards include narrow roads, sharp curves, insufficient shoulders and no separation between traffic directions. Dangers such as these can easily lead to a loss of control.

Even something like the pavement dropping off a few inches at the road's edge can deliver tragic consequences. Says James Jeffery III, a traffic engineer based in Los Gatos, Calif., "You panic and throw the steering wheel the other way." Such overcorrecting can quickly land you in oncoming traffic.

Bad Signs, Poor Markings

We've all seen places where a lack of signs, or a confusing assemblage of too many, causes a moment of confusion. So we brake abruptly to read the signs or, says AAA's Dinh-Zarr, swerve to catch our exit, cutting across lanes without looking properly, which could easily cause a collision.

At nighttime, signs and pavement markings increase in importance. "Many of the visual cues you need to drive safely are often more difficult to see," says Greg Schertz, a Federal Highway Administration safety engineer based in Denver. In our examination of fatal accidents with no record of driver error, one out of every three took place after dark.

Part of the problem is that many roads, especially rural ones, haven't had their signs and markings updated in a long time. "They're faded, unclear, missing," Steed says. "Pavement markings that don't show up in the rain are just as hazardous. In a heavy storm, you could easily leave your lane and not know it."

Pedestrian Peril

It had just finished raining on the night of December 19 [2002] and Lawrence Sullivan, 56, was on his way toward Mansfield, Massachusetts. Heading north on Route 140 in his Honda Civic, Sullivan was traveling under the speed limit when he felt and heard a sudden impact. Slamming on the brakes, he came to a stop. Moments later, he realized that he had struck two pedestrians: a 78-year-old woman and her son, 45.

The average 75-year-old needs at least three times more light that a 25-year-old to see the same objects.

The two had left Alberto's Italian Kitchen and were walking to a mobile home park across the street. After investigating, police declined to press charges. "There was nothing the driver did that was incorrect or improper," says patrolman David Ruskey. "Several other witnesses said they couldn't see the pedestrians either."

That section of Route 140 has no sidewalk, crosswalks or intersections. What's more, the road is only lit on one side— the side opposite Alberto's. "People walk across that busy road every day, all day long," says Alberto's manager Brett Becker. "There needs to be a crosswalk or something."

But that would be no guarantee of safety. Though most pedestrians are hit while jaywalking, 1,700 people were killed in crosswalks from 1998 to 2001. Studies show that many pedestrians enter crosswalks with a false sense of security, believing that vehicles will stop no matter what. They often don't.

Lighting at crosswalks is frequently to blame. Put a pedestrian in dark clothing at a poorly lit intersection on a dark night and you're asking for trouble, says Dinh-Zarr. And aging baby boomers will once again be at a disadvantage as their eyesight deteriorates: The average 75-year-old needs at least three times more light than a 25-year-old to see the same objects.

Dean Johnson has started the Sandy Johnson Foundation to educate drivers about dangerous roads and to ensure that the problems are corrected. "Our highway system should be constructed in such a way that it does not cause simple driver error to turn catastrophic," he says. Johnson plans to create an online database of dangerous intersections nationwide.

AAA's Dinh-Zarr sees traffic safety as a public health issue. "It's the big challenge for the 21st century," she says. "We must view crashes as deadly diseases and work to eradicate them before they take hold. The safety of our roads themselves remains the missing piece of our vaccine."

5

Seniors Who Stop Driving Decline Faster Than Those Who Still Drive

SeniorJournal.com

SeniorJournal.com is a popular news and information Web site for senior citizens.

A 2006 study by researchers at Johns Hopkins University found that seniors who continue driving are less likely to enter nursing homes or assisted living facilities than those who give up their car keys. The study found that non-drivers had four times the risk of entering long-term care than drivers. The researchers concluded that losing the ability to drive has a real health impact on seniors. As those who cannot drive become more isolated, the likelihood that they will need help increases. In addition, the absence of another driver in the home doubles the risk of institutionalization. The researchers say they hope their findings will encourage communities to provide alternative transportation for seniors who cannot drive.

Although the slower driving habits of some seniors often steam impatient younger motorists, researchers at Johns Hopkins School of Medicine have found that elders who stay behind the wheel are less likely to enter nursing homes or assisted living centers than those who have never driven or who have given up driving altogether.

The Hopkins study findings, published in the July [2006] issue of the *American Journal of Public Health*, included exten-

SeniorJournal.com, "Senior Citizens Who Give Up Driving May Take Express Lane to Nursing Home," July 19, 2006. Reproduced by permission.

sive interviews conducted over a 10-year period with 1,593 seniors between 65 and 84 years of age who live in the small, Eastern Shore town of Salisbury, Md.

"We are not recommending continuation of driving for seniors who are a threat to themselves or others on the road," said Ellen Freeman, Ph.D., an epidemiological researcher now working with the Johns Hopkins Wilmer Eye Institute and the study's lead author. "Instead, we hope that understanding the very real health impact that losing the ability to drive has on seniors will encourage families to plan contingencies to assist elderly members with transportation issues."

Independence Means Quality of Life

The researchers also pointed out that losing the ability to drive poses an especially significant hardship to seniors living in isolated rural areas or any place without good, accessible public transportation for the elderly.

"We set out to learn whether or not the loss of driving ability played a measurable role in an older person's eventual need for long-term care," said Sheila West, Ph.D., a professor of ophthalmology at the Johns Hopkins School of Medicine. "The independence that accompanies a driver's license and car has long been linked anecdotally to a better quality of life for seniors."

The absence of other drivers in the home doubled the risk of entering long-term care.

Freeman and others on the Hopkins team stressed that from both a personal and public policy standpoint, the need is greater than ever to figure out what best and safely helps older people keep an independent lifestyle. "The average annual cost of nursing home admission is $69,000, and the price tag associated with entry into assisted living is roughly

$30,000," she noted. "That's a public policy issue of huge dimensions as our population ages."

Driving Is Just One Part of Mobility Issue

"This probably isn't so much about the process of driving but rather the larger issue of mobility as it relates to a person's independence," added Freeman. "When someone becomes a shut-in due to the loss of their primary transportation, the likelihood that they will require living assistance categorically increases."

Non-drivers across the entire age group studied had four times the risk of long-term care entry compared to drivers, and the absence of other drivers in the home doubled the risk of entering long-term care. Nine percent of those studied entered long-term care for three months or more. By the end of the study, 29 percent of men and 58 percent of women had no other drivers in the household, and 22 percent of people who were driving at the beginning of the study reported that they stopped driving during the study.

Freeman and her colleagues said their study methods took into account and factored out many other causes of "long-term care entry," including age, race, marital status and such health problems as frailty, dementia and stroke damage. There were no significant differences in outcomes between men and women.

More Research Is Needed

"These findings point to the importance of research into how to keep seniors driving and independent as long as is safely possible," said West, director of the Johns Hopkins Initiative for Translational Research on Driving and the study's senior author.

Salisbury, the site of the 10-year study, is a semirural town of about 40,000 people. Freeman cautioned that because no formal public transportation system was available to the residents of the town, the findings of the study should only be interpreted as meaningful for communities of similar size that also lack public transportation infrastructure.

6

More Seniors than Younger Drivers Die in Auto Accidents

SeniorJournal.com

SeniorJournal.com is a popular news and information Web site for senior citizens.

A 2006 study by the National Institute on Aging found that drivers sixty-five and older are significantly more likely to die when they are involved in an automobile accident than a younger person is. Despite driving slower and wearing their seat belts more often, older drivers were still much more likely to be injured or die than even a middle-aged driver. The typical senior driving fatality involves a sober driver with his seat belt on pulling out in front of another car in broad daylight. The study's authors offer several recommendations to help reduce seniors' injuries and deaths behind the wheel.

Senior citizens will die in car accidents at a higher rate in the years ahead as America's 75 million baby boomers age, grow more frail and continue to drive, according to a new study. Already, seniors age 65 and over are second-most likely to die in car accidents, after young people aged 15–24, according to a National Institute on Aging report on America's elderly, "65+ in the United States: 2005," released March 9 [2006].

"In general, older people are more susceptible to injury than younger people," said Richard Kent, assistant professor of mechanical and aerospace engineering at U.Va.'s [University of Virginia's] School of Engineering and Applied Science and co-author of the study.

"As the population ages, the ratio of women to men also changes, going from 1-to-1 for young people to 100 women for every 35 men by age 85. And, women tend to be more frail than men, making them more susceptible to injury."

Kent studied the characteristics of car accidents and the nature of injuries sustained by older drivers in a research project titled "On the Fatal Crash Experience of Older Drivers."

Award-Winning Study

The resulting paper, co-authored with Basem Henary, research associate, mechanical and aerospace engineering at U.Va. and Fumio Matsuoka, project manager for vehicle safety, Vehicle Engineering Division, Toyota Motor Corp., Japan, was named the Best Scientific Paper for 2005 by the Association for the Advancement of Automotive Medicine in Barrington, Ill., an organization dedicated to the prevention and control of injuries from motor vehicle accidents.

The researchers' goal was to identify unique aspects of older-driver crashes—in particular, the body region injured, the severity of the crash and the circumstances surrounding fatal crashes in which they were involved—with an eye to identifying patterns that could be used in developing new technologies to assist seniors in driving safely.

"The archetypical elderly driver fatality involves a belted, sober driver pulling into the path of an oncoming vehicle during the day and dying several days after a collision."

The researchers studied police reports on thousands of vehicle accidents for the years 1992–2002. They examined the accidents and injuries for three groups of drivers: young adults (16–33), middle-aged adults (34–64), and seniors (65 and older).

The Findings

The researchers' findings included:

- Drivers 65 and over killed in car accidents were significantly more likely to die of a chest injury (47.3 percent vs. 24.0 percent in the youngest group)

- Younger drivers were more likely to die of a head injury (22.0 percent vs. 47.1 percent in the oldest group)

- Older drivers were more likely to die at a date after the crash date ("delayed death")

- Frailty or pre-existing health conditions played a significant role in the deaths of the older group, but not in the younger group (50.0 percent of the deaths of the older group vs. 4.3 percent of the younger drivers' deaths)

- Despite driving at lower average speeds than younger and middle-aged drivers, and a greater likelihood of wearing seat belts, older drivers were more likely to be injured or die in an accident than younger drivers.

According to the paper, published in the September 2005 *Annual Proceedings of the Association for the Advancement of Automotive Medicine*: "The archetypical elderly driver fatality involves a belted, sober driver pulling into the path of an oncoming vehicle during the day and dying several days after a collision of moderate severity.

"Pre-existing health issues are often related to the death. In contrast, the archetype for a 30-45 year-old driver fatality involves an unbelted, impaired driver losing control of his/her vehicle at night and dying during an extremely severe, single-vehicle crash."

Ways to Reduce Risks for Seniors

The study recommended that government and industry officials consider changes that would help reduce seniors' injuries and deaths from motor vehicle collisions. Areas deserving of attention included: roadway design, road signage, vehicle controls and active and passive safety systems.

Researchers also identified technological developments that could help older drivers. These included seat belts that would limit the force of a crash on a driver's body, crash-avoidance systems, technologies that would prevent elderly drivers from crossing the centerline or pulling into an intersection without having the right-of-way.

7

Seniors Who Cannot Drive Grapple with Isolation

Gordon Dickson

Gordon Dickson is a staff writer for the Fort Worth Star-Telegram, *a daily newspaper in Texas. His work appears in various publications throughout the country via a newswire service.*

Seniors who can no longer drive feel an acute loss of freedom and become increasingly isolated. They make fewer trips to the doctor, shop less frequently, and make 65 percent fewer trips to church or to visit friends and relatives. Minority or low-income seniors—and those in rural areas—are among those most likely to be stranded without transportation. Public transportation is of little help to most seniors because it is designed for young, able-bodied people, not for older adults who may have health and mobility problems. Communities need to plan for the future of their aging residents and invest in supportive transportation options for seniors who can no longer drive.

R uth Nichols belongs to the Grapevine Garden Club, but doesn't remember the last time she attended a function.

She recently gave up driving because pressing the brake pedal hurt her right leg. The 79-year-old widow rarely leaves the house now, except for a van ride to bone cancer treatments every few weeks.

Nichols is among 7 million Americans over age 65 who don't drive and those numbers are expected to nearly double in the next two decades.

A study warns that older Americans without access to public transportation are becoming increasingly isolated. These nondrivers make fewer trips to the doctor and lose contact with friends, relatives and churches.

Nichols can't deny the loss of freedom.

"I had some great automobiles in my time—a T-bird, a Rally Sport Camaro," she said on the way to her doctor's appointment. She rode in a low-fare van operated by Northeast Transportation Service.

"Now, I've got a 1988 Buick Regal in the garage," she said. "I guess I will sell it. Somebody's going to get a great car."

More than one in five Americans over age 65 doesn't drive.

Texas is one of the worst areas in the nation for senior citizens who have surrendered their car keys, according to the study released by the Surface Transportation Policy Project, a Washington-based group that lobbies for increased spending on buses, trains and other forms of transit.

Public Transportation Is Designed for Younger Adults, Not Seniors

Even in areas where there are plans to improve public transportation, the routes typically are designed for working-age adults, said Anne Canby, president of the group. For example, commuter rail trains that are served by park-and-ride lots may be of little help to residents who can't drive to the station.

"We need to get serious about planning for the needs of older Americans," Canby said. "We need to be thinking about the link between where this population lives and where it wants to go. In suburban areas, it's going to require some real figuring out."

More than one in five Americans over age 65 doesn't drive, according to the study, which is titled "Aging Americans: Stranded Without Options." Of those, more than half say that on a given day they simply stay home in part because of a lack of transportation options.

"When seniors don't have an option to drive any more, they don't like to ask others for a ride," Canby said. "They feel like a burden on their children. That precedes the isolation factor."

The study, which is based on results of a nationwide survey conducted in 2001 by the U.S. Transportation Department, also found that older nondrivers:

- Make 15 percent fewer trips to the doctor, 59 percent fewer trips to shops and restaurants, and 65 percent fewer trips to church or to visit relatives.

- Use public transportation widely in places where it's available. In 2001, nondriving seniors took 310 million trips on public transportation.

- Are more likely to be stranded if they are minorities, low-income or rural residents.

"I don't want to go to New York. I just want to go to church," said Louise Carbonaro, 83, a Roanoke [Texas] widow. "All I can say is, 24 hours alone is hard."

Recommendations for Congress

The study recommends that Congress spend more money on public transportation, and that cities across the United States do a better job planning for seniors' needs. Also recommended are improvements to roads, sidewalks and bicycle paths.

Hubert Chandler Sr., 86, who lives in southwest Fort Worth, has no plans to stop driving. He pays close attention to his driving habits, to ensure he's in firm control at all times.

He hopes to remain behind the wheel well into his 90s. He admits to being overly cautious, often waving other drivers through stop signs to ensure that he isn't involved in an accident.

"I go to the bank. I go to the Food Mart on Vegas Trail. I play the lotto," he said. "If I couldn't drive, it would be sad indeed."

Seniors Miss Spontaneous Freedom Most

For many senior citizens, the issue is not whether they can get to a doctor's appointment, but whether they can enjoy a vestige of the freedom they once had behind the wheel.

"We conducted a survey, and among people age 50-plus, there was more concern about having access to social interaction and recreation than there was about access to doctors," said Candice Carter, associate state director for AARP [American Association of Retired Persons], a group that advocates for senior citizens' rights.

"We know a tremendous population boom of people age 50-plus is coming, and yet communities haven't prepared for this."

Nichols paused for a moment when asked if there is a place she wishes she could still go spontaneously—like she did when she was behind the wheel of her T-Bird, Camaro or Buick.

"The zoo," she said finally. "Wouldn't that be wonderful?"

8

Senior Drivers Should Be Screened More Thoroughly Than Others

Katherine Siggerud

Katherine Siggerud is the director for physical infrastructure issues at the U.S. Government Accountability Office.

Although most states have toughened their license renewal procedures for senior drivers, there are no reliable and valid assessment screening tools specifically for older drivers. In addition, no state uses a screening tool to evaluate physical or cognitive functions, the biggest areas of potential concern for this age group. The National Highway Traffic Safety Administration (NHTSA) is doing extensive research and developing new tools to help states more reliably assess the abilities of older drivers. The NHTSA believes that refining screening and assessment tools is the most important work that can be done to address the safety of senior drivers.

To make roads safer for older drivers, FHWA [Federal Highway Administration] has recommended practices—such as using larger letters on signs, placing advance street name signs before intersections, and improving intersection layouts—for the design and operation of roadways that make them easier for older drivers to navigate. FHWA is also continuing research to demonstrate the effectiveness of these practices. While these practices are designed to address older

Katherine Siggerud, Older Driver Safety; Report to the Special Committee on Aging, U.S. Senate, Washington, DC: Government Accountability Office, 2007.

drivers' needs, their implementation can make roads safer for all drivers. States have, to varying degrees, incorporated FHWA's older driver safety practices into their design standards, implemented the practices in roadway operation and maintenance activities, trained technical staff in applying the practices, and coordinated with local agencies to promote the use of the practices. Following are the actions taken by the 51 DOTs [Departments of Transportation] we surveyed in the states and District of Columbia:

- 24 states reported including about half, most, almost all, or all of FHWA's practices in their state design guides.

- 51 states reported implementing advance traffic control warning signage on approaches to intersections.

- 12 states reported they had trained about half, most, almost all, or all of their technical staff.

- 38 states reported they had held sessions on older driver issues with local governments.

There is insufficient evidence on the validity and reliability of any driving assessment or screening tool.

FHWA also provides federal highway funding that states may use to implement projects that address older driver safety. While older driver safety projects are eligible for federal highway funding, state DOTs generally place a higher priority on and commit more of their limited resources to other projects—such as railway/highway intersection safety projects, roadside hazard elimination or mitigation projects, road intersection safety projects, and roadway departure projects—that more broadly affect all drivers. Although older driver safety is not the primary focus of these projects, the projects may incorporate FHWA's recommended practices to improve older driver safety.

How States Make Assessments

More than half of the states have implemented assessment practices to support licensing requirements for older drivers that are more stringent than requirements for younger drivers. These requirements generally involve more frequent renewals (16 states), mandatory vision screening (10 states), in-person renewals (5 states), and mandatory road tests (2 states) for older drivers. In addition, all states accept physician reports and third-party referrals of concerns about drivers, while 36 states use medical advisory boards to assist licensing agencies in assessing driver fitness. . . .

However, the assessment practices that state licensing agencies use to evaluate driver fitness are not comprehensive. For example, our review of state assessment practices indicates that all states screen for vision, but we did not find a state with screening tools to evaluate physical and cognitive functions. Furthermore, the validity of assessment practices used by states is largely unknown. While research indicates that in-person license renewal is associated with lower crash rates—particularly for those aged 85 and older—other assessment practices, such as vision screening, road tests, and more frequent license renewal cycles, are not always associated with lower older driver fatality rates. According to NHTSA [National Highway Traffic Safety Administration], there is insufficient evidence on the validity and reliability of any driving assessment or screening tool. Thus, states may have difficulty discerning which tools to implement.

Developing More Comprehensive Assessment Practices

NHTSA, supported by the NIA [National Institute on Aging] and by partner nongovernmental organizations, has promoted research and development of mechanisms to assist licensing agencies and other stakeholders—medical providers, law enforcement officers, social service providers, family members—in better identifying medically at-risk individuals; assessing their driving fitness through a comprehensive evaluation of visual, physical, and cognitive functions; and enabling their driving for as long as safely possible. In the case of older drivers, NHTSA recognizes that only a fraction of older drivers are at increased risk of being involved in an accident and focuses its efforts on providing appropriate research-based materials and information to the broad range of stakeholders who can identify and influence the behavior of at-risk drivers. Initiatives undertaken by NHTSA and its partner organizations include:

Model Driver Screening and Evaluation Program. Initially developed by NHTSA in partnership with AAMVA [American Association of Motor Vehicle Administrators] and supported with researchers funded by NIA—the program provides a framework for driver referral, screening assessment, counseling, and licensing actions. The guidance is based on research that relates an individual's functional abilities to driving performance and reflects the results of a comprehensive research project carried out in cooperation with the Maryland Motor Vehicle Administration. Recent research supported under this program and with NIA grants evaluated a range of screenings related to visual, physical, and cognitive functions that could be completed at a licensing agency and may effectively identify drivers at an increased risk of being involved in a crash.

Physician's Guide to Assessing and Counseling Older Drivers. Developed by the American Medical Association to raise awareness among physicians, the guide cites relevant literature and expert views (as of May 2003) to assist physicians in judging patients' fitness to drive. The guide is based on NHTSA's earlier work with the Association for the Advancement of Automotive Medicine. This work—a detailed literature review—summarized knowledge about various categories of medical conditions, their prevalence, and their potential impact on driving ability.

Countermeasures That Work: A Highway Safety Counter-measure Guide for State Highway Safety Offices. Developed with the Governors Highway Safety Association, this publication describes current initiatives in the areas of communications and outreach, licensing, and law enforcement—and the associated effectiveness, use, cost, and time required for implementation—that state agencies might consider for improving older driver safety.

Virtual reality driving simulation is a potentially viable means of testing that could more accurately identify cognitive and motor impairments than could on-road tests.

NHTSA Web site. NHTSA maintains an older driver Web site with content for drivers, caregivers, licensing administrators, and other stakeholders to help older drivers remain safe.

New Screening Tools

NIA is supporting research on several fronts in studying risk factors for older drivers and in developing new tools for driver training and driver fitness assessment.

- A computer-based training tool is being developed to help older drivers improve the speed with which they process visual information. This tool is a self-administered interactive variation of validated training techniques that have been shown to improve visual processing speed. The tool is being designed as a cost-effective mechanism that can be broadly implemented, at social service organizations, for example, and made accessible to older drivers.

- Driving simulators are being studied as a means of testing driving ability and retraining drivers in a manner that is more reliable and consistent than on-road testing. Virtual reality driving simulation is a potentially viable means of testing that could more accurately identify cognitive and motor impairments than could on-road tests that are comparatively less safe and more subjective.

- Research is ongoing to evaluate the impacts of hearing loss on cognitive functions in situations, such as driving, that require multitasking. Results of the research may provide insights into what level of auditory processing is needed for safe driving and may lead to development of future auditory screening tools.

- Studies that combine a battery of cognitive function and road/driving simulator tests are being conducted to learn how age-related changes lead to hazardous driving. Results of these studies may prove useful in developing screening tests to identify functionally-impaired drivers—particularly those with dementia—who are at risk of being involved in a crash and may be unfit to drive.

NHTSA is also developing guidelines to assist states in implementing assessment practices. To date, NHTSA's research and model programs have had limited impact on state licensing practices. For example, according to NHTSA, no state has implemented the guidelines outlined in its *Model Driver Screening and Evaluation Program*. Furthermore, there is insufficient evidence on the validity and reliability of driving assessments, so states may have difficulty discerning which assessments to implement. . . . In its plan NHTSA notes that the most important work on older driver safety that needs to occur in the next 5 years is refining screening and assessment tools and getting them into the hands of the users who need them.

9

Taking Keys Away from Senior Drivers Is a Challenge for Families

Janice Gallagher

Janice Gallagher is a regular contributor to The Kentucky Post, *a daily newspaper in Covington, Kentucky.*

Older drivers often experience failing eyesight, slowing reflexes, and diminishing cognitive ability. Unfortunately, the law is little help in getting seniors who should not be driving off the road. Consequently, families, doctors, and seniors themselves must be responsible for ensuring public safety. Seniors can take many steps to ensure their safety, as well as the safety of other drivers. Driver refresher training can help, as can limiting trips, not driving at night or in heavy traffic, and traveling only familiar routes. Seniors can also learn to recognize the warning signs of dangerous driving and give up driving on their own once they occur. Ultimately, though, families may need to take keys away from their senior members and physicians may need to report unsafe drivers to the Department of Motor Vehicles.

One morning last fall [2004] Boone County [Kentucky] police got a call from a passing driver that an elderly man was driving the wrong way on Ky. 18. Police tracked down the man, who turned out to be 83, in a parking lot and confronted him.

He denied the incident.

So police told the man's family, who also confronted him. When he became angry, the family didn't know what to do. So the subject was dropped and never broached again.

Knowing when to hang up the car keys—or when to pressure an elderly driver to put them away—isn't an easy decision for seniors and their loved ones. It's a frequent topic of elderly caregiver support groups and among seniors themselves, said Pat Schneider, who said she often sees families and individuals distraught over the dilemma, which can pit issues of public safety against freedom and quality of life for seniors.

On the one hand, driving equals independence and self-sufficiency. Take that away and the consequences can be demoralizing, said Schneider, a community education specialist for Senior Services of Northern Kentucky.

"It takes away freedom and their identity," she said. "People have the right to be independent for as long as they can be."

Ceasing to drive means decreased access to social activities, medical services, shopping, church and other important aspects of people's lives.

On the other hand, it's a hard fact that driving skills diminish as health fails, and public safety must be considered.

It's left up to the elderly, their doctors and their families to ensure safety.

Aging Brings Physical Changes

With the natural aging process comes decreased visual, mental and physical abilities and slower reflexes. Side effects from prescription drugs, as well as existing and developing health ailments, also can make it harder for elderly people to drive safely. Arthritis, Parkinson's disease, the effects of a stroke or devices such as a pacemaker might cause an irregular heartbeat or dizziness, which can make driving dangerous, Schneider said.

Accident statistics show that older drivers generally are as safe as other age groups until they reach 75, when they typically begin to have more accidents. But even before then, safety becomes a concern: The crash rate per mile driven begins to increase at age 65, and motor vehicle injuries are the leading cause of injury-related deaths for people ages 65 to 74.

Experts say it's true that mature drivers aren't as reckless as young and new drivers, but many are betrayed by failing eyes and reflexes. The crux is discovering the point at which those physical skills become a problem.

Unfortunately, the law is little help, at least in Kentucky and Ohio. Both states treat all drivers alike, whether they're 28 or 98, and allow periodic renewal of licenses with no restrictions. In contrast, about half of the states have some special requirements for older drivers, such as vision tests. But even only a few of those states require stricter measures like medical reports or road tests.

As a result, it's left up to the elderly, their doctors and their families to ensure safety.

Age Alone Is Not a Sign of Ability

The issue is not only complex but urgent. With aging baby boomers expected to live longer and be more active than previous generations, more elderly drivers will be on the roads. By 2030, more than one in five Americans will be 65 or older and one in 11 of those individuals will be 85 or older.

But it's important to recognize that age alone isn't a good indicator of driving ability, said Jenelen Dulemba, executive director of PrimeWise, a resource program for seniors and their families run out of St. Elizabeth Medical Centers [in Northern Kentucky].

"I cringe when someone looks at the driving issue by age," she said. "It's an individual's ability. It's not usually the average senior (who has problems), but a person with health problems."

The goal should be not to revoke licenses but to help people keep driving as long as they safely can, Schneider said. "There are ways to do it and it can be done but the matter must be handled with kindness and persistence," she said.

Elderly drivers are often victims of stereotypes.

Organizations such as AARP [American Association of Retired Persons] offer driver refresher training, which has the added advantage of often reducing insurance premiums. Other groups show seniors how to make adjustments to their car, such as making seats higher to improve vision, that increase safety. Others suggest ways for seniors to regulate themselves, such as not driving at night or during rush hours or on expressways.

[In 2006] 4,500 Kentuckians over age 50 completed the AARP driving safety course designed to show aging drivers how to self-monitor their skill level, said Don Pendleton, AARP's driving safety coordinator in Kentucky. The eight-hour course, for example, advises elderly drivers to plan a trip before leaving the house, to stay on familiar streets and to take routes that avoid risky spots such as ramps and left turns.

Groups Urge Education and Self-Monitoring

Pendleton suggests seniors follow smart driving tips and become aware of warning signs, which include being nervous or fearful while driving, having difficulty staying in one lane, driving too fast or too slow, [encountering] frequent "close calls," accidents and minor scrapes, getting lost more often, [experiencing] confusion and violating signals and road signs.

But Pendleton said elderly drivers are often victims of stereotypes.

"Older people are more conscientious and attuned to what is going on on the road. What happens is that a lot of stats look bad and get publicity," Pendleton said. "It's the 25-year-old with a cell phone to his ear that is the unsafe driver."

But in the end, hazardous drivers who continue to get behind the wheel may be forced to give up his or her license.

In Kentucky, a physician, a relative or caregivers can alert the county driver's license bureau if an elderly person appears to be driving erratically and won't give up the keys. Individuals also often report themselves, according to Mike Goins, spokesman for the Kentucky Transportation Cabinet.

Licenses are then suspended while the driver is given time to prove his or her competence.

The state Medical Advisory Board has the authority to identify drivers with physical or mental impairments that impede the ability to drive. Last year [in 2003] 1,350 cases were reported to the board.

On average about 70 driver's licenses are suspended each month, but elderly drivers and others who might have driving impairments represent only a portion of that number, Goins said.

Thus it's difficult to enumerate just how big of a problem those drivers are.

10

The National Agenda Should Include Senior Driving Issues

Ezra Ochshorn

Ezra Ochshorn is a social worker at the Florida Mental Health Institute in Tampa.

There is no simple or single solution to the problems associated with seniors and driving. A comprehensive national agenda is required to address the growing body of senior driving issues. Such an effort should include heavy investment in public transportation, better roadway and infrastructure design, more education on the dangers of driving with decreased capabilities, the development of reliable screening tools to replace today's simplistic driving tests, the establishment of a restricted license program to allow curtailed driving privileges, and better transportation services for the six hundred thousand seniors who stop driving each year. Failing to spend the money on these initiatives now will have a much greater cost—both in dollars and lives lost—in the future.

For an elderly couple I know who live in rural Florida, driving represents far more than everyday independence and freedom. It means survival. With no one else to get their food and medicine, and no public transportation, he drives while she tells him where to go. Both are approaching 80, the wife paralyzed from a stroke, the husband legally blind.

Since an 86-year-old motorist plowed into a farmers' market in Santa Monica, Calif., in July [2003]—killing 10 and in-

Ezra Ochshorn, "Needed: Aging-Driver Policy," The *Christian Science Monitor*, September 3, 2003, p. 9. © 2003 The *Christian Science Monitor*. Reproduced by permission of the author.

juring dozens—some commentators have suggested older drivers are an irresponsible menace with no business on public roadways. Given the growth in the senior population, the national debate on how—or whether—to regulate driving privileges for the elderly is really only just beginning.

Most older motorists I met during eight years of working in hospitals were safe drivers who restricted their own travels, such as driving only in the daytime. Indeed, when it comes to deadly road behavior—speeding, driving while intoxicated, running red lights, using cellphones, road rage—research by the government, the AAA [Automobile Association of America], and the insurance industry shows the majority of perpetrators are younger drivers.

Age Is a Risk Factor

That said, advanced age definitely is a risk factor in driving safety. Problems with vision, hearing, reaction time, medication use, cognitive impairment, and physical ailments can spell roadway disaster. I also have known elderly drivers who are in deep denial about their diminished driving capacity. While people over 70 comprise about 10 percent of licensed drivers, federal transportation data show they are involved in 13 percent of all fatal traffic accidents. On a per-mile-driven basis, they have higher accident rates than all but the youngest drivers.

The problem is an example of America's reluctance to face its rapidly 'graying' demographics.

Furthermore, it is often elder drivers themselves who don't survive crashes. Seniors who are physically vulnerable are far more likely than younger drivers to die of a comparable injury, according to the American Medical Association. By age 85, their auto fatality rate is nine times that of drivers aged 25 to 69.

Something needs to be done, most people agree. But what?

Most important, we must dismiss the notion of a single, simple solution. Elder driving cannot be viewed in a vacuum—nor can the lack of concrete action taken to address the issue.

The problem is an example of America's reluctance to face its rapidly "graying" demographics.

Ways to Address the Senior Driving Issue

Rather than quick fixes, we need a comprehensive national agenda:

- First and foremost, invest heavily in public transportation to reduce dependence on automobiles. It is an inhumane recipe for disaster to insist that a senior stop driving without offering an affordable, reliable transportation alternative.

- Design roadways and cars to accommodate the reduced vision and slower reflexes of elder drivers (safety measures that would aid younger drivers as well). For example, add larger road signs, wider highway lanes, and bigger car mirrors.

- Publicize the warning signs of diminished road competence for aging drivers so they and their families can better identify them and take action before tragedies occur.

- Increase physician education about medical conditions that can impair older patients' driving skills. Though it could strain doctor-patient trust, physicians should be required to refer seniors for further evaluation when a clear risk to personal and public health exists.

- Develop comprehensive, objective, technologically sophisticated driver evaluations to replace simplistic vision and road tests. Given the tremendous variation between individuals and degree of impairment, it should not be age or diagnosis alone that determines whether drivers can keep their licenses.

- Expand driver rehabilitation programs and laws that grant restricted licenses, allowing seniors to keep driving as long as safely possible.

- Address the adjustment problems faced by the 600,000 older persons forced to stop driving each year—a number that will mushroom in coming decades. Significant social isolation and depression are common among these people, and that, in turn, can trigger major health problems.

Some will argue that these recommendations are too costly to implement. I suggest that unless large-scale action is taken now to accommodate our rapidly aging population, we will pay far more in years to come, both in dollars and in lost lives.

11

Better Transit Programs Would Help Seniors Give Up Driving

Helen Kerschner and Joan Harris

Helen Kerschner is president and chief executive officer of the Beverly Foundation, a nonprofit organization that works to enhance mobility and transportation for older people through research and education. Joan Harris has been with the U.S. Department of Transportation for more than sixteen years, mainly working in the areas of policy and research to improve road safety and transportation choices for seniors.

Today's older adults are very likely to live past the time when they can drive safely, but they will still need to go places. Transportation is the key to maintaining quality of life for seniors. Supplemental Transportation Programs (STPs) are one of the best ways to serve the nondriving senior population. STPs differ from regular public transportation in that they may include an escort for the senior during the trip, help boarding and exiting the vehicle, door-to-door assistance, or even door-through-door assistance to help seniors get safely situated inside their homes. There are many different types of STPs, and cities nationwide are trying different things. Well-developed STP offerings in a community will help seniors drive less or give up driving altogether.

Helen Kerschner and Joan Harris, "Better Options For Older Adults," *Public Roads*, vol. 70, March–April 2007. U.S. Department of Transportation, Federal Highway Administration.

Older adults need to go to a variety of life-sustaining destinations—the doctor, grocery store, perhaps an exercise class. They *want* to go to any number of life-enriching locales—the library, recreation center, church, a volunteer job. By reaching these destinations, they continue to participate fully in society as workers, volunteers, family members, friends, and consumers. Unfortunately, not everyone is able to stay mobile as they age.

According to a 2004 study by a national nonprofit advocacy organization, the Surface Transportation Policy Project, 20 percent of adults age 65 and older do not drive. Of that age group, 54 percent stay home on any given day (compared to 9 percent of people of all ages who drive). Reduced mobility translates into 15 percent fewer trips to the doctor for nondriving older people and 65 percent fewer trips for social, family, and religious purposes.

Communities and service providers across the nation experience the transportation challenges facing older adults, especially the very old who may need personal assistance. Many communities and organizations nationwide have created Supplemental Transportation Programs (STPs) for seniors to add to traditional transportation services, which often do not meet the needs of nondriving seniors.

Although some STPs may provide transportation to people with disabilities and even to the general population, most were created to serve seniors, especially those who are frail and in need of assistance. Similar to traditional services, they offer transportation to a variety of destinations. Most STPs also supply "supportive transportation" in the form of door-to-door and door-through-door assistance. They may even arrange for an escort to stay with a passenger at a destination. In many instances the STP's driver or escort is a volunteer.

STPs are among a mix of transportation options beginning to take shape for seniors. "Public transportation systems around the country are working with their communities so that older adults have options to go shopping, visit family and friends, volunteer, or go to the doctor," says William Millar, president of the American Public Transportation Association (APTA). "Programs should constitute a family of services that best meet the needs of older adults and are the most cost effective for the community. Depending on their physical needs and destinations, older adults would get around by bus, train, community center van, medical ambulance, or another senior who volunteered to drive them. Seniors would call one number to find out the best way to get to their destinations or look it up and schedule it right on the Internet."

Attention at the Top

The White House Conference on Aging (WHCoA) takes place once every 10 years. It now has a 50-year history of bringing together policymakers, planners, service providers, and older Americans to make policy recommendations to Congress and the President on the full range of aging-related issues.

At the . . . conference, held in December 2005, some 1,200 delegates appointed mainly by Governors and Members of Congress were asked to name 50 top policy priorities. Assuring availability of transportation options for seniors was voted number 3 among the 50 resolutions, ahead even of those addressing Medicare and Medicaid. This top ranking represents a fundamental shift from prior WHCoAs and further reflects a growing understanding among aging-service professionals, transportation experts, and seniors themselves that transportation is the key to maintaining quality of life for older Americans.

Giving Up the Keys

Concerns about older drivers' safety, coupled with the need to maintain mobility in the community, are responsible for much of the growing interest in transportation options. Although most older adults are safe drivers, many choose to limit their driving to surface streets and no freeways, their immediate neighborhoods, and daylight hours. Others give up their keys because they fear driving or have a physical, mental, or financial limitation. As a result, many outlive their ability to drive.

According to "Driving Life Expectancy of Persons Aged 70 Years and Older in the United States," by Daniel J. Foley et al. in the *American Journal of Public Health*, both men and women are likely to live beyond the time that they can drive safely, as much as 6 years for men and about 10 for women. During that period, they will lose the independence of the personal automobile and become dependent on alternative transportation.

The United States is at a critical juncture in ensuring that older Americans have the mobility and independence that have been the hallmark of the baby boomer generation.

In years past, family members or friends were expected to help older adults who no longer drove. But today in the United States, multigenerational families are no longer common. Therefore, fewer stay-at-home caregivers are available to fill the driving gap. Many nondriving seniors depend instead on public and community-based transportation services, such as fixed route, circulator route, paratransit, dial-a-ride, taxi service, and human service transit programs. However, many communities do not offer these services, and even where they are available, older adults may be unable to use them because of the physical conditions that forced them to give up driving in the first place.

Target Population

The projected rapid expansion of the 65-plus age group in the next 20 years presents major challenges to society in terms of consumer markets, workforce composition, and productive retirement. Transportation poses one of the greatest challenges, and meeting the needs of the 85-plus group is the most difficult task within that challenge. That group may need special assistance that traditional public transportation systems, particularly fixed route and paratransit services, were not designed to provide. In contrast, 65- to 85-year-olds often serve their communities and help older adults by being volunteer drivers.

According to the U.S. Census Bureau, in 2000 there were more than 35 million Americans age 65 and older. That number is expected to increase beyond 71 million by 2030. Although the number of "young old" (ages 65–85) will increase dramatically, the "old old" (age 85-plus) will show even greater growth. For example, 10.9 percent of the population was age 65–85 and 1.5 percent was age 85 and older in the year 2000. These numbers will increase to 17.0 percent and 2.6 percent, respectively, by 2030, and to 15.7 percent and 5.0 percent in 2050.

"The United States is at a critical juncture in ensuring that older Americans have the mobility and independence that have been the hallmark of the baby boomer generation," says APTA's Millar.

[The] 'Five A's of Senior-Friendly Transportation' include availability, accessibility, acceptability, affordability, and adaptability.

This presents communities with an emerging challenge. They can join the two sides of aging—the "young wellderly," who may have the time and energy to contribute as paid or volunteer drivers, with the "old elderly," who are transportation-dependent and need community-based options.

Need for Senior-Friendly Options

Many in the aging-service community note the difficulty if not impossibility of stopping driving if no alternative is available. Simply having options, however, may not be sufficient, as transportation services must be "senior-friendly." The Beverly Foundation in Pasadena, CA, has conducted extensive research to arrive at five principles defining the issue. These "Five A's of Senior-Friendly Transportation" include availability, accessibility, acceptability, affordability, and adaptability.

Meeting these senior-friendly requirements can be difficult for public transit and Americans with Disabilities Act (ADA) paratransit services (special-demand responsive systems for people with disabilities), and even for human-service organizations that provide transportation to seniors. Restrictions on funding and the distance to destinations often limit the available transportation to a single purpose, or to certain days of the week or hours of the day.

Supportive transportation includes door-to-door and door-through-door assistance and often involves escorts at the destination—all essential elements of senior-friendly service.

Consequently, transportation often is unavailable for "quality of life" destinations. A senior may be able to find community transportation to a doctor's appointment but may be unable to get to a bridge group or the hairdresser. Costs for paid staff, vehicles, equipment, and insurance can limit dramatically the ability of a transportation service to do more than provide fixed-route or curb-to-curb service for older adults. Further, drivers without proper training who treat seniors with insensitivity can mean the difference between seniors getting where they need to go and choosing to stay at home.

Perhaps the major reason that many traditional transportation providers find it so difficult to serve the "old old" is that their services simply were not designed to meet the special needs of this population. Providers may drive passengers from one point to another, but their services generally do not include helping passengers into and out of vehicles, or staying with passengers at destinations. On the other hand, supportive transportation includes door-to-door and door-through-door assistance and often involves escorts at the destination—all essential elements of senior-friendly service for many older adults. In many instances the only means of providing this support is by involving volunteer drivers and escorts

Local Communities Take the Lead

STPs were first identified in a joint effort by the Beverly Foundation and the AAA [Automobile Association of America] Foundation for Traffic Safety in Washington, DC. "Given the expected [increase in the number of] seniors over the age of 65, it is essential that our society provide transportation alternatives to folks who can no longer safely drive," says Peter Kissinger, president and chief executive officer of the AAA Foundation. "To that end, STPs will continue to play a vital role, and we have been delighted to collaborate with the Beverly Foundation to develop resources for organizations to use in planning and implementing them in their communities."

The two foundations initiated the partnership in 2000 with a national survey of STPs. In annual surveys from 2000 to 2005, the groups documented 492 STPs throughout the United States. Because of that research, STPs now are recognized as an approach with national significance.

Although some STPs are large and costly to operate, the majority are relatively small and inexpensive. Annual budgets range from $1,000 to $9.8 million, with a median of $58,000. Thirty-three percent of STPs target rural areas, 44 percent use automobiles as their transportation vehicles, and 49 percent can provide escort services. Although 46 percent of the STPs charge fees, 75 percent draw on grant revenue, and 23 percent tap into funding from Federal, State, or local government for some or all of their support. (The figures do not add to 100 percent because STPs typically draw on a mix of funding sources.) Although driver recruitment and funding are said to be major challenges, the fact that the STPs average 24 years in service suggests they are remarkably successful in sustaining their operations.

Volunteer Drivers

Transportation services that use paid drivers report that the salaries generally constitute 50 percent or more of the budgets. Vehicle ownership is another major expenditure. Volunteer drivers and their vehicles enable many STPs to serve older adults adequately. Although some volunteers are reimbursed for mileage, the savings realized from not paying driver salaries or purchasing vehicles are substantial. Also, volunteer drivers generally are committed to being helpful and thus are able to provide the door-to-door, door-through-door, and destination assistance needed.

In the study of STPs, 55 percent used volunteer drivers and 76 percent provided door-to-door service. The 2004 and 2005 surveys documented 179 volunteer-driver STPs and 728 volunteer drivers.

The data from those surveys suggest some major differences among volunteer-oriented STPs. Budgets for volunteer STPs range from $1,000 to nearly $4.4 million, with a median of $23,500. Seventy-four percent of volunteer STPs are in rural areas, 84 percent use the vehicles of volunteer drivers, 97 percent provide door-to-door service, and most say that drivers act as escorts. Although only 13 percent charge fees, 71 percent draw on grants, 62 percent use rider donations, and 18 percent tap tax revenues for some or all of their support. Volunteer-driver programs are a somewhat newer phenomenon than STPs in general, but they appear to be successful in sustaining their operations, because statistics show that they average 17 years in operation to date.

Volunteer drivers have been described as the engine that drives not only the vehicle but also the program. Of the 728 volunteer drivers in the database, 63 percent are age 65 and older, 51 percent have graduated from college, 65 percent have household incomes of $30,000 or more, and 67 percent are married. Fifty-five percent have been volunteer drivers for more than 3 years. Many volunteers report that getting to know passengers is one of their greatest sources of satisfaction, and a large number indicate that they hope such a program will be there for them when they are no longer able to drive.

Examples of STPs

STPs vary widely, as indicated by the following descriptions of programs across the nation:

West Austin Caregivers. Located in Austin, TX, West Austin Caregivers is a Robert Wood Johnson Foundation-*Faith in Action* program sponsored by local congregations. Caregivers began operating in 1985 with an urban service area of 59.6 square kilometers (23 square miles), and it now has an annual budget of around $65,000. It provides assistance to older adults but emphasizes transportation for frail elders. The transportation service is provided by 100 volunteer drivers who use their own vehicles, and the program schedules curb-to-curb, door-to-door, and door-through-door assistance. In 2005 caregivers provided 4,860 rides to older adults and supported its activities with donations from riders, community organizations, and foundations. A consortium of eight volunteer driver programs that serve greater Austin jointly market the services, recruit volunteer drivers, and raise funds to support their individual and group activities.

Transportation Reimbursement and Information Program (TRIP). TRIP began operating in 1993, serving 18,647.9 square kilometers (7,200 square miles) in Riverside County, CA, with an $802,946 annual budget. The program is a stand-alone service with organizational and financial links to the local agency on aging and the county transportation service. Although it recruits some volunteer drivers, TRIP is organized to recruit riders who then recruit their own drivers. Thus the agreement for transportation is made between the rider and driver, and it is not necessary for staff to schedule rides. Many drivers act as escorts and even assist riders with daily activities. In 2005, TRIP provided 82,406 rides (and more than 700,000 rides during 13 years of operation) with support and funding from the Riverside County Transportation Commission.

Prairie Hills Transit. Located in Spearfish, SD, Prairie Hills started service in 1990 as a senior transportation program and evolved into a community transportation provider, with a service area of 25,428.5 square kilometers (9,818 square miles) and a budget of $986,000. The program provides medical and general-purpose trips, many of which cover 120.7 kilometers (75 miles) one way. The needs of the senior population make it necessary to provide some door-to-door and through-the-door help. The program operates 21 vehicles with 21 paid drivers. It uses volunteer drivers mainly to take people to church on Sunday. In 2004, Prairie Hills provided 91,565 rides and funded its services primarily from State department of transportation (DOT) funds, aging-services money, Medicaid, funds from city and county fare box revenues, and donations and fund-raising activities.

Ride Connection. Located in Portland, OR, Ride Connection was organized as a network of transportation providers that receives public funding to complement the ADA service available through the municipal corporation (Tri-Met) that provides public transportation for much of the three local counties. With a service area of 9,580 square kilometers (3,699 square miles) and a budget of $5 million, Ride Connection is a volunteer transportation service run for and by older adults.

It links responsive transportation with the needs of older adults and people with disabilities. In 2005 the service connected a network of more than 30 service providers, scheduled more than 358,749 rides for 10,447 people, and involved 233 paid drivers and 374 volunteers in providing personalized and accessible door-to-door services. Ride Connection receives the majority of its grant funding from the Oregon DOT and Tri-Met.

OATS, Inc. Located in Columbia, MO, OATS began as a senior transportation program in 1971 and evolved into a community provider with a service area of 131,157 square kilometers (50,640 square miles) and an $18.2 million budget. OATS provides reliable transportation for transportation-disadvantaged Missourians so they can live independently in their own communities. OATS fulfills its mission by providing group transportation to seniors, people with disabilities, and the public. It operates a fleet of 622 vehicles and a driver force of 530 paid drivers. In 2005, OATS provided more than 1.5 million rides and funded its services through private contracts, State general revenue, Older Americans Act funding, and multiple Federal Transit Administration programs.

Who Is Doing What?

More and more people and organizations in the fields of health care, law enforcement, driver licensing, social and aging services, and transportation safety are leading the expansion and improvement of transportation alternatives. Many of these groups now offer training, technical assistance, financial support, research, community events, and other services that increase awareness and broaden transportation options.

For instance, the Community Transportation Association of America advocates for senior mobility in several areas, such as nonemergency medical transportation, employment transportation, and rural and public transportation. The association promotes universal design in transportation, provides funding and technical assistance to small communities and nonprofits as they set up new or expanded transportation services for seniors, and pursues other activities that instill "senior-friendliness" in transportation.

The AAA Foundation for Traffic Safety organization funds a number of research and demonstration projects to improve older road user safety, such as signal timing, in-vehicle technologies, and medications and driving. Some . . . projects are devoted to enhancing alternatives to driving. . . . The American Public Transportation Association [www.apta.com] is working to increase senior mobility on public transit through several avenues, such as development of best practices guidelines for transit providers. For example, the Easy Rider program encourages public transportation providers to improve the senior-friendliness of their services.

AARP [American Association of Retired Persons] has offered driver improvement courses for more than 25 years, and millions of drivers have attended. More recently AARP has moved beyond driver safety to focus also on mobility alternatives. AARP is active with local metropolitan planning organizations, ensuring that the voice of the age 50-plus consumer is included when transit decisions are made. Under the banner of its Social Impact Agenda, AARP wants to ensure that "complete streets" are available to all, so that when driving is no longer an option, individuals may walk, ride bicycles, or use transit. The most recent revision to the classic AARP driver safety curriculum now includes a section on transitioning out of driving.

Many large professional organizations, such as the Gerontological Society of America (GSA) and American Society on Aging (ASA), are seeing significant increases in members interested in transportation and aging. Within these associations, special-interest groups dedicated to enhancing safe and effective senior transportation have formed recently, and the annual conferences now feature a growing number of sessions that reflect the broad range of transportation projects currently under way. These groups have joined with other organizations to improve driver safety (the CarFit and DriveWell programs, both by ASA, for example) and have published research, white papers, and special issues of journals. See www.geron.org/interest.htm for GSA and www.asaging.org for ASA. . . .

Alternative transportation programs are about enabling people to reduce or stop driving when they need to do so. . . . And ultimately, they are about adding life to the years that have been added to life.

Why It Matters

Many transportation planners understand that they cannot build their way out of congestion, so one of their goals is to provide a range of transportation choices such as carpools, buses, and light rail that people will actually use. But in providing choices for older people who no longer drive, planners also must make sure that the choices are senior-friendly.

Transit and transportation officials, human service planners, and transportation providers who are exploring ways of meeting the transportation needs of older Americans increasingly are recognizing the senior-friendliness of the STP. Although it can take considerable time and extensive involvement by numerous groups and community leaders to organize an STP, the cost may be lower than other alternatives, and the result will be a senior-friendly service that older people will actually use.

Alternative transportation programs are about enabling people to reduce or stop driving when they need to do so. They are about providing a safe transportation alternative and ensuring the availability of low-cost, senior-friendly options. They are about enabling older adults to secure the basic necessities. They are about community involvement and community support. And ultimately, they are about adding life to the years that have been added to life.

Organizations to Contact

The editors have compiled the following list of organizations concerned with the issues presented in this book. The descriptions are derived from materials provided by the organizations. All have publications or information available for interested readers. The list was compiled on the date of publication of the present volume; the information provided here may change. Be aware that many organizations take several weeks or longer to respond to inquiries, so allow as much time as possible.

AARP
601 E St. NW, Washington, DC   20049
(800) 424-3410
e-mail: member@aarp.org
Web site: www.aarp.org

AARP, formerly known as the American Association of Retired Persons, is a nonpartisan association that seeks to improve the aging experience for all Americans. AARP publishes the magazine *Modern Maturity* and the newsletter *AARP Bulletin*. It also operates the 55 Alive Driver Safety Program, a motor vehicle safety course for senior citizens. The AARP Web site offers a wealth of information about seniors and driving, including online skills assessments, research reports, issue statements and congressional testimony on transportation issues.

Administration on Aging (AOA)
330 Independence Ave. SW, Washington, DC   20201
(202) 619-0724 • fax (202) 357-3555
e-mail: aoainfo@aoa.gov
Web site: www.aoa.dhhs.gov

The AOA works with a number of organizations, senior centers, and local service providers to help older people remain independent. AOA's publications include fact sheets on issues such as age discrimination, Alzheimer's disease, and safe driving. Additional publications are available through AOA's National Aging Information Center.

Advocates for Highway and Auto Safety
750 First St. NE, Suite 901, Washington, DC   20002
(202) 408-1711 • fax: (202) 408-1699
e-mail: advocates@saferoads.org
Web site: www.saferoads.org

Advocates for Highway and Auto Safety is an alliance of consumer, health, and safety groups and insurance companies that seek to make America's roads safer. The alliance advocates the adoption of federal and state laws, policies, and programs that save lives and reduce injuries, including those related to seniors and driving. On its Web site, the organization publishes fact sheets, press releases, polls, and reports, as well as links to legislative reports and testimony on federal legislation involving traffic safety.

The Alzheimer's Association
919 North Michigan Ave., Suite 1100
Chicago, Illinois   60611-1676
(800) 272-3900 • fax: (312) 335-1110
e-mail: info@alz.org
Web site: www.alz.org

The Alzheimer's Association is committed to finding a cure for Alzheimer's and helping those affected by the disease. The association funds research into the causes and treatments of Alzheimer's disease and provides education and support for people diagnosed with the condition, their families, and caregivers. Position statements and fact sheets about dementia and driving are available at its Web site.

American Geriatrics Society (AGS)
350 Fifth Ave., Suite 801, New York, NY   10118
(212) 308-1414 • fax (212) 832-8646

e-mail: info@americangeriatrics.org
Web site: www.americangeriatrics.org

AGS is a professional organization of health-care providers that aims to improve the health and well-being of all older adults. AGS helps shape attitudes, policies, and practices regarding health care for older people. The society's publications include the book *The American Geriatrics Society's Complete Guide to Aging and Health*, the magazine *Journal of the American Geriatrics Society* and *The AGS Newsletter*. These publications feature occasional articles regarding driving safety or research and other senior transportation issues.

American Society on Aging
833 Market St., Suite 511, San Francisco, CA   94103-1824
(415) 974-9600 • fax: (415) 974-0300
e-mail: info@asaging.org
Web site: www.asaging.org

The American Society on Aging is an organization of health-care and social service professionals, researchers, educators, businesspersons, senior citizens, and policy makers that is concerned with all aspects of aging and works to enhance the well-being of older individuals. Its publications include the bimonthly newspaper *Aging Today* and the quarterly journal *Generations*. The summer 2003 issue of *Generations*, is devoted entirely to senior transportation and community mobility issues.

Family Caregiver Alliance (FCA)
80 Montgomery St, Suite 1100, San Francisco, CA   94104
(800) 445-8106 • fax: (415) 434-3508
e-mail: info@caregiver.org
Web site: www.caregiver.org

Founded in 1977, Family Caregiver Alliance is a community-based nonprofit organization that serves the needs of families and friends providing long-term care at home. FCA offers programs at the national, state, and local levels to support and assist caregivers, and is a public voice for caregivers through education, services, research, and advocacy. Its Web site offers a wide range of information on caregiver issues and resources, including numerous fact sheets, policy papers, and other publications, some of which focus on driving and alternative transportation for seniors.

Global Action on Aging (GAA)
777 UN Plaza, Suite 6J, New York, NY   10017
212-557-3163 • fax: 212-557-3164
e-mail: globalaging@globalaging.org

GAA, based in New York at the United Nations, reports on older people's needs and potential within the global economy. It advocates by, with, and for older persons worldwide. Its Web site includes reports, issue updates, and articles, including many about transportation and driving.

Insurance Institute for Highway Safety
1005 N. Glebe Rd., Suite 800, Arlington, VA   22201
(703) 247-1500 • fax: (703) 247-1588
Web site: www.hwysafety.org

The Insurance Institute for Highway Safety is a nonprofit research and public information organization formed by auto insurers. The institute conducts research to find effective measures to prevent motor vehicle crashes. On its Web site, the institute publishes information on the results of its research and makes it available for free download. Of particular note is "Older Drivers Up Close: They Aren't Dangerous Except Maybe to Themselves," which appears in *Status Report*, vol. 36, no. 8.

International Federation on Ageing (IFA)
425 Viger Ave. W, Suite 520, Montréal, Québec
   H2Z 1X2
(514) 396-3358 • fax: (514) 396-3378
e-mail: ifa@citenet.net
Web site: www.ifa-fiv.org

The IFA is a private nonprofit organization that brings together over 150 associations that represent or serve older persons in fifty-four nations. IFA is committed to ensuring the dignity and empowerment of older persons. It publishes the quarterly journal, *Ageing International*, and a monthly newsletter for its members, *Intercom*.

National Association of Area Agencies on Aging (N4A)

1730 Rhode Island Ave. NW, Suite 1200
Washington, DC   20036
(202) 872-0888 · fax (202) 872 0057
Web site: www.n4a.org

The N4A is the umbrella organization for the 655 area agencies on aging in the United States. Its mission is to help older people and those with disabilities live with dignity and choices in their homes and communities for as long as possible. The N4A Web site provides links to Area Agencies on Aging in all states as well as to other government organizations that serve seniors. It also acts as a portal for the Eldercare Locator, a national toll-free number to assist older people and their families find community services for seniors anywhere in the country. The N4A has a program that promotes older driver safety, and it advocates for better transportation options for seniors.

National Council on the Aging (NCOA)

300 D St., SW, Suite 801, Washington, D.C.   20024
(202) 479-1200 • fax: (202) 479-0735
e-mail: info@ncoa.org
Web site: www.ncoa.org

The NCOA is an association of organizations and professionals dedicated to promoting the dignity, self-determination, well-being, and contributions of older people. It advocates business practices, societal attitudes, and public polices that promote vital aging, including best practices regarding senior driving and transportation. NCOA's quarterly magazine, *Journal of the National Council on the Aging*, provides tools and insights for community service organizations.

National Highway Traffic Safety Administration (NHTSA)

1200 New Jersey Ave. SE, West Building
Washington, DC 20590
(888) 327-4236
Web site: www.nhtsa.gov

The NHTSA is a federal government agency responsible for saving lives, preventing injuries, and reducing economic costs due to road traffic crashes, through education, research, safety standards, and enforcement activity. Its Web site offers extensive research reports and hundreds of articles about older drivers and the various transportation issues seniors face.

National Motorists Association (NMA)

402 W. Second St., Waunakee, WI 53597-1342
(608) 849-6000 • fax: (608) 849-8697
e-mail: nma@motorists.org
Web site: www.motorists.org

Founded in 1982, the NMA advocates, represents, and protects the interests of North American motorists. The NMA does not support frequent retesting or age-based restrictions of senior drivers. The NMA believes a system should be put in place to evaluate the driving competency of motorists who, though an objective screening criteria, come to the attention of the licensing authority. On its Web site, the NMA provides access to a wide range of articles and reports, including "Dealing with Elderly Drivers," "Edlerly Driver Information," and "Back to School for Elderly Drivers."

The Seniors Coalition

9001 Braddock Rd., Suite 200, Springfield, VA 22151
(703) 239-1960 • fax: (703) 239-1985
e-mail: tsc@senior.org
Web site: www.senior.org

The Seniors Coalition, which positions itself as an alternative to the AARP, is a nonpartisan education and issue advocacy organization that represents the concerns of America's senior citizens. The coalition publishes *The Advocate* magazine, which sometimes features articles about senior driving and transportation.

Traffic Injury Research Foundation (TIRF)
171 Nepean St., Suite 200, Ottawa, ON
  K2P 0B4
  Canada
(613) 238-5235 • fax: (613) 238-5292
e-mail: tirf@trafficinjuryresearch.com
Web site: www.trafficinjuryresearch.com

Founded in 1964, TIRF is an independent road safety institute that seeks to reduce traffic-related deaths and injuries in Canada by designing, promoting, and implementing effective programs and policies based on sound research. TIRF publications include brochures, the *TIRF Bulletin*, and technical reports. One recent project initiative focused specifically on elderly drivers, culminating in the report "Understanding Crashes Involving Elderly Drivers," which is available on the TIRF Web site.

Bibliography

Books

Jon Burkhardt, Arlene Berger, and Adam McGavock
The Mobility Consequences of the Reduction or Cessation of Driving by Older Women. Washington DC: Federal Highway Traffic Safety Administration, 1996.

Xuehao Chu
The Effects of Age on the Driving Habits of the Elderly. Washington DC: Technology Sharing Program, Research and Special Programs Administration, U.S. Dept. of Transportation, 1994.

Ari Houser
Older Drivers and Automobile Safety. Washington DC: AARP Public Policy Institute, 2005.

William Mann
Community Mobility: Driving and Transportation Alternatives for Older Persons. Glasgow, Scotland: Haworth, 2006.

Joan Yuhas McGowan
Driving While Elderly. Ringoes, NJ: Blue Tree Books, 2004.

Harry Moody
Aging: Concepts and Controversies, 3rd edition, Thousand Oaks, CA: Pine Forge, 2000.

Linda Rhodes
The Complete Idiot's Guide to Caring for Aging Parents. New York: Alpha, 2000.

John Peter Rothe | *The Safety of Elderly Drivers: Yesterday's Young in Today's Traffic.* Edison, NJ: Transaction, 1990.

Ken Smith | *The Senior Driver's Guidebook: How to Keep Driving Longer and Survive in the 21st Century.* Twin Cities, MN: Five Star, 1999.

Patricia Smith, Mary Kenan, Mark Edwin Kunik, and Leeza Gibbons | *Alzheimer's for Dummies*, Hoboken, NJ: Wiley, 2003.

U.S. Department of Transportation | *Transportation for a Maturing Society*, Washington, DC: Author, 1997.

Rachelle Zukerman | *Eldercare for Dummies*, 1st ed. Hoboken, NJ: Wiley, 2003.

Periodicals

Dale Buss | "What Should We Do About Grandma's Driving?" Edmunds.com, 2006.

James J. Callahan Jr. | "Giving the Elderly Options on Independent Living," *Boston Globe.* November 24, 2002.

Howie Carr | "Age Slows Us All Down Except for Licensed Geezers," *Boston Herald*, October 17, 2007.

Consumer Affairs	"Demented Drivers a Growing Traffic Menace; Doctors Enlisted to Watch for Signs of Dementia in Patients," *Consumer Affairs*, December 26, 2006.
Matthew Craft	"Risk of Fatal Crashes Rises in the Elderly, Data Show," *Seattle Post-Intelligencer*, July 18, 2003.
Marrecca Fiore	"Exercise May Help Elderly Drivers," *Foxnews.com*, June 24, 2007.
Marc Fisher	"Too Old to Drive? D.C. Prefers Not to Know," *Washington Post*, May 23, 2007.
Fisher Center for Alzheimer's Research	"Driving and Dementia: A Dangerous Mix," Fisher Center for Alzheimer's Research Foundation, www.alzinfo.org, August 8, 2003.
Robert B. Friedland	"Caregivers and Long-Term Care Needs in the 21st Century: Will Public Policy Meet the Challenge?" Issue Brief, Long-Term Care Financing Project, Georgetown University, Washington, DC, 2004.
David Grabowski, Christine Campbell, and Michael Morrisey	"Elderly Licensure Laws and Motor Vehicle Fatalities," *Journal of the American Medical Association*, vol. 291, pp. 2840–2846, 2004.
Andrew Haas	"A Crash Course for the Elderly," *New York Times*, Op-Ed, July 17, 2006.

Insurance Institute for Highway Safety — "Older Drivers Up Close: They Aren't Dangerous Except Maybe to Themselves." *Status Report*, vol. 36, no. 8, September 8, 2001.

Eli Lehrer — "Grandpa Can So Drive: Motorists Between 55 and 70 Are Actually the Safest Drivers on the Road," *National Review*, July 18, 2003.

Mei-Li Lin et al. — Special Issue on Driving and the Elderly, *Journal of Safety Research* vol. 34, no 4, 2005.

Larry Lipman — "America Facing a Crisis of Elderly Non-Drivers," Cox News Service, April 13, 2004.

Alan Martin, Lucy Balding, and Desmond O'Neill — "Are the Media Running Elderly Drivers off the Road?" *British Medical Journal* vol. 330, no. 7487, p. 368, February 12, 2005.

Norra MacReady — "It's Hard to Tell Elderly, Stop Driving Your Car," *Internal Medicine News*, August 1, 2005.

June Maxam — "Bizarre Senior Driving Accident Shows Danger of Elderly Drivers," *North Country Gazette*, October 24, 2005.

James McNight — "The Freedom of the Open Road—Driving and Older Adults," *Generations*, American Society on Aging, Summer 2003.

Kathleen Murphy   "Elderly Drivers Pose Growing Challenge for States and Auto Insurers," *Insurance Journal*, June 7, 2004.

Francine Russo   "Driving Us Crazy: New Help for Older People Who Are Shaky Behind the Wheel—and Their Children," *Time*, August 15, 2005.

Daniel Wood   "Road Rules: Helping the Elderly Drive Safely," *The Christian Science Monitor*, February 19, 2004.

Index

A

AAA (American Automobile
Association), 37
    Foundation for Traffic Safety,
    12, 75, 80
    Michigan road hazard im-
    provements, 38
AARP. See American Association
of Retired Persons
Accident statistics
    age comparison, 21, 23–26
    cause of deaths, 62, 66
    Fatality rates, 12, 13, 62.68
    research findings/
    recommendations, 47–49
    road hazards, 37–38
    senior citizens, 7–8, 12–13, 30
    side impact crash, 14
ADA (Americans with Disabilities
Act), 74
Advisory boards, medical, 56, 64
Age
    discrimination, 8, 63–64, 84
    driving limitations, 12, 13
    shift, demographic, 29–30
"Aging Americans: Stranded With-
out Options" study, 52
Alternative transportation. See
Transportation alternatives
American Association of Motor
Vehicle Administrators, 57
American Association of Retired
Persons (AARP), 8–9, 15, 22
    aarp.org (web site), 9
    driver improvement courses,
    63, 80
    Driver Safety Program, 9, 16,
    32

findings, 31
    Social Impact Agenda, 34, 80
American Journal of Public Health,
9, 16, 42, 71
American Medical Association, 7,
57, 66
American Public Transportation
Association (APTA), 70, 80
American Society on Aging (ASA),
80, 81
Americans with Disabilities Act
(ADA), 74
Annual Proceedings of the Associa-
tion for the Advancement of Auto-
motive Medicine, 48
APTA (American Public Transpor-
tation Association), 70, 80
Apta.com (web site), 80
Arthritis, 22, 61
ASA (American Society on Aging),
80, 81
Assessment of older drivers
    California pilot plan, 17
    Florida, 30
    Maryland, 17–18
    needed improvements, 56–58
    new screening tools, 58–59
Association for the Advancement
of Automotive Medicine, 47, 57
Auditory screening tools, 59
Austin, Rory, 14

B

Baby boomers
    increasing numbers, 21, 37
    mobility of, 31–32, 62
    statistics, 30, 46, 73
    See also Senior drivers

Baer, Richard, 16

Baldick, Elizabeth Jane, 15

Becker, Brett, 41

Bohuslav, Ken, 39

Bolka, Katie, 11–12, 13, 16, 18–19

Bolka, Rick, 19

C

California driver assessment pilot plan, 17

Canby, Anne, 51, 52

Car accidents. *See* Accident statistics

Carbonaro, Louise, 52

Caregivers, stay-at-home, 71

CarFit program, 81

Carnegie Mellon University, 12, 14

Carter, Candice, 53

Cataracts, 21

Center for the Study and Improvement of Regulation (Carnegie Mellon University), 14

Chandler, Hubert, 52

Cognitive abilities in seniors
attention span, 7
degeneration, 13, 14, 21, 61
dementia, 22
depression, 22
inadequate evaluation, 56, 67
Memory loss, 14
testing, 17–18, 57

Community Transportation Association of America, 79

Commuter rail trains, 51

Compensation measures, of senior drivers, 22, 26–28

Coordination, 7
See also Physical abilities in seniors

Corona, John, 19

Countermeasures That Work: A Highway Safety Countermeasure Guide for State Highway Safety Offices, 58

D

Dallas incident, 11–12, 15, 16–17, 18

Dangers posed by senior drivers, 23–26, 28

Davis, Robert, 11–19

DeBarros, Anthony, 11–19

Dementia, 22

Department of Motor Vehicles (DMV), 22, 24

Department of Transportation (DOT)
alternative transportation funding, 78–79
older driver assessment, 55–56

Depression, 22

Dial-a-ride services, 72

Dickson, Gordon, 50–53

Dinh-Zarr, Bella, 37, 40, 41

Discrimination, age, 8, 63–64, 84

DMV (Department of Motor Vehicles), 22, 24

Driver rehabilitation programs/laws, 68

Driver Safety Program (AARP), 9, 16, 32

Drivers. *See* Senior drivers; Teenage drivers

Drivers licenses. *See* License renewals; Licensing/testing issues

DriveWell program, 81

Driving laws, state level
first level of defense, 19
inconsistency, 13, 62
individual requirements, 17–18
Kentucky, 62, 64

Ohio, 62, 64
stricter for elderly, 20–21, 22, 24
Texas, 13, 19
"Driving Life Expectancy of Persons Aged 70 Years and Older in the United States" (Foley), 71
Driving simulators, 58–59
Dulemba, Jenelen, 62

E

Early warning system, 17, 67
Easy Rider program, 80
Evaluation of older drivers, 67–68
Exams, behind-the-wheel, 13, 19

F

Faigin, Barbara, 14
Fatality rates, 12, 13, 62.68
Fay, Brian, 15
Federal Highway Administration (FHWA)
    older driver safety practices, 54–55
    state implementation of assessment tools, 55–56
Federal Transit Administration programs, 79
Fischbeck, Paul, 14
Florida
    driver assessment, 30
    Highway Patrol, 15
    incident, 8, 21
    increase in seniors, 30
Foley, Daniel J., 71
Ford Motor Company, 9
Freeman, Ellen, 43

G

Gallagher, Janice, 60–64
Geron.org (web site), 81

Gerontological Society of America (GSA), 80
Ginzler, Elinor, 15
Glaucoma, 21
Goins, Mike, 64
Gorman, Carolyn, 16
Governors Highway Safety Association, 13, 58
Grapevine Garden Club, 50
Grimes, Elizabeth, 11–12, 15, 16–17, 18–19

H

Harris, Joan, 69–82
Harsha, Barbara, 13, 17
Heart disease, 22
Henary, Basem, 47

I

Identifying unsafe drivers
    driving knowledge test, 17
    early warning system, 17, 67
    failures, 17
    levels of defense, 19
    new techniques, 58–59
    road tests, 13, 56
    state assessment methods, 56–58
    written tests, 22
Illinois, licensing/testing procedures, 8
In-person renewals, 56
Increase in senior citizen population, 21, 37
Insomnia, 22
Insurance Information Institute, 16
Insurance Institute for Highway Safety (IIHS), 13, 17, 18
Insurance rates, 16
Isolation of seniors, 50–53

J

Jeffery, James, 39
John Hopkins School of Medicine, 9, 42–45
Johnson, Dean, 36, 41
Johnson, Sandy, 35
Journal of Safety Research, 14
Journal of the American Geriatrics Society, 18
Journal of the American Medical Association, 13

K

Karp, Hal, 35–41
Kent, Richard, 46
Kentucky
    driving laws, 62
    Transportation Cabinet, 64
Kerschner, Helen, 69–82
Kissinger, Peter, 75
Knowledge test, 17

L

Laanso, Eero, 9
Lawsuit, (Bolka), 16–17
Levels of defense, 19
License renewals
    frequency of, 56
    in-person appearances, 8, 13, 17, 22, 56
    strictness for elderly, 54
Licensing/testing issues
    Florida, 18
    Illinois and New Hampshire, 8, 13
    inadequacies, 54, 68
    Kentucky and Ohio, 62, 64
    procedures, 12, 13, 19, 65
    revoking licenses, 17, 64
Long-term care and mobility, 44

Loss of driving ability, reasons/consequences
    declining health, 42–43
    fear for survival, 65
    feelings of isolation, 31–32, 50–53
    loss of independence, 44, 61
    loss of mobility, 73
    quality of life, 43
Loughran, David, 20–28

M

Macular degeneration, 21
Malouf, Peter, 19
Maryland Motor Vehicle Administration, 57
Maryland study, driver assessment, 17–18
Matsuoka, Fumio, 47
Medical issues
    advisory boards, 56, 64
    effects of medication, 7, 14, 22, 61
    focus abilities, 14
    medical responsibilities, 56
    research, 21
Memory loss, 14
Millar, William, 70, 73
Miller, Kim, 15
Miller, Richard, 38
Mobility
    importance of, 44–45, 73, 79, 85
    long-term care, 44
    loss, 31, 50, 70
    maintaining, 10, 34, 69, 71–72, 80
Model Driver Screening and Evaluation Program, 57, 59
Motion range, 7
Multimodal transportation systems, 32–33

N

National Highway Traffic Safety Administration (NHTSA), 14, 36, 37, 56
  assisting older driver assessment, 59
  Countermeasures That Work: A Highway Safety Countermeasure Guide for State Highway Safety Offices, 58
  Model Driver Screening and Evaluation Program, 57, 59
  Physician's Guide to Assessing and Counseling Older Drivers, 57
  web site, 58

National Institute on Aging, 46, 56, 58–59

National Older Driver Research and Training Center, 7

New Hampshire, licensing/testing procedures, 8

Nichols, Ruth, 50, 51, 53

Northeast Transportation Service, 51

Northern Kentucky
  Senior Services, 61
  St. Elizabeth Medical Centers, 62

O

OATS, Inc., 79

Ochshorn, Ezra, 65–68

Ohio Department of Transportation (ODOT), 36

Ohio driving laws, 62, 64

Older Americans Act, 79

"On the Fatal Crash Experience of Older Drivers" (Kent, Richard), 47–49

P

Paratransit services, 72, 73, 74

Parkinson's disease, 61

Pendleton, Don, 63

Perry, Rick, 19

Physical abilities in seniors
  compensation measures, 22, 26–28
  degeneration, 13, 21–22, 61–62
  lack of evaluation, 56
  publicized warning signs, 30, 67
  reaction time diminishment, 7, 14, 22, 61

Physician's Guide to Assessing and Counseling Older Drivers, 57

Prager, David, 11–12, 18

Prairie Hills Transit, 78

PrimeWise, 62

R

Rader, Russ, 18

Reaction time diminishment, 7, 14, 22, 61

Recommendations, for senior drivers, 67–68

Reflexes, 14, 30, 60, 62, 67

Responsibility, medical, 56, 67

Ride Connection, 78–79

Ride-share programs, 10

Riverside County Transportation Commission, 78

Road hazards, 37–41
  improvements, 67
  Ohio incident, 35–36
  Wood County, Texas incident, 38–39

Road tests, 22
  Illinois/New Hampshire requirements, 13

state mandatory, 56

See also Identifying unsafe drivers

Roadway improvements, 67

Roadway Safety Foundation (RSF), 37

Robert Wood Johnson Foundation, 77

Rollovers, single-vehicle, 14

Ruskey, David, 41

S

Sandy Johnson Foundation, 41

Santa Monica incident, 7–8, 14, 21, 65

Schertz, Greg, 40

Schneider, Pat, 61, 63

School of Engineering and Applied Science (University of Virginia), 46

Screening tools, new, 58–59

Seabury, Seth, 20–28

Senior citizens

compensation measures, 26–28, 30

growth of population, 21, 29–30, 37

relative exposure of, 23

safe drivers, 11, 20, 22–28, 30, 63

self-regulation by, 15, 16, 18, 22

See also Baby boomers

Senior drivers

conscientiousness of, 11, 20, 22–26, 63

dangerousness of, 23–26, 28

evaluation improvement, 67–68

fatality rates, 12, 13

insurance rates, 16

recommendations to assist, 67–68

remedial training and education, 23, 63

self-risks of, 26, 27–28

See also Identifying unsafe drivers; Loss of driving ability, reasons/consequences

"Senior-Friendly Transportation," 73–75

Senior Services of Northern Kentucky, 61

Senior vans, 10

SeniorJournal.com, 42–49

Siggerud, Katherine, 54–59

St. Elizabeth Medical Centers (Northern Kentucky), 62

State driving laws. *See* Driving laws, state level

Stay-at-home caregivers, 71

Steed, Diane, 37, 39, 40

Stroke, 61

Sullivan, Lawrence, 40

Supplemental Transportation Programs (STPs), 70–82

OATS, Inc., 79

Prairie Hills Transit, 78

Ride Connection, 78–79

Transportation Reimbursement and Information Program, 77–78

West Austin Caregivers, 77

Surface Transportation Policy Project

"Aging Americans: Stranded Without Options" study, 51–53

findings, 70

Sutton, Chad, 38

Sutton, Rita, 39

Sweden, multimodal transportation system, 32–33

T

Teenage drivers
    insurance rates, 16
    safety concerns about, 64, 66
    single-vehicle rollovers, 14
Texas Department of Transportation (TxDOT), 39
Texas Legislature, 13, 19
Thames, Byron, 29–34
The Beverly Foundation, 74, 75
Toyota Motor Corp., Vehicle Engineering Division, (Japan), 47
Training tools, computer-based, 58
Transportation alternatives
    commuter rail trains, 51
    drivers/escort volunteers, 73, 74, 76–77
    funding, 33–34, 74
    ineffective public transportation, 51–52
    multimodal transportation systems, 32–33
    need for, 67–68, 71
    public transportation, 51–52
    senior vans, 10
    Supplemental Transportation Programs, 70–82
Transportation Reimbursement and Information Program (TRIP), 77–78

Transportation systems, Swedish multimodal, 32–33
Tri-Met, 78
TxDOT (Texas Department of Transportation), 39

U

U.S. Census Bureau, 7, 12–13

V

Vision issues
    declining vision, 7, 14, 21–22, 61
    vision testing, 13, 17, 19, 22, 56

W

Weller, George Russell, 14
West, Sheila, 43
West Austin Caregivers, 77
White House Conference on Aging (WHCoA), 71
Wilmer Eye Institute (Johns Hopkins School of Medicine), 43

Z

Zakaras, Laura, 20–28